CREEPY BUT TRUE

TALES FOR THE CAMPFIRE

JOSHUA WARREN AND
ANDREA SAARKOPPEL

ROSEN
PUBLISHING

New York

This edition published in 2016 by:
The Rosen Publishing Group, Inc.
29 East 21st Street
New York, NY 10010

Library of Congress Cataloging-in-Publication Data

Warren, Joshua P.
Creepy but true: tales for the campfire/Joshua P. Warren, with Andrea
Saarkoppel.
    pages cm.—(True tales of terror)
Originally published: It was a dark and creepy night. Pompton Plains :
Career Press, c2014.
Includes bibliographical references and index.
ISBN 978-1-4994-6152-7 (library bound)
1. Occultism. 2. Parapsychology. 3. Curiosities and wonders. I. Title.
BF1411.W325 2015
130—dc23

                                                            2014050326

Manufactured in the United States of America

First published as *It Was a Dark and Creepy Night: Real-Life Encounters with the
Strange, Mysterious, and Downright Terrifying* by New Page Books/Career Press,
copyright © 2014 Joshua P. Warren

CONTENTS

INTRODUCTION

Imagine you're in a huge forest, sitting next to a crackling campfire on a cool, dark night. In front of you are the warm, flickering flames, twisting and dancing hypnotically. And behind that fire, in a dark, wooded space, is a rugged log. This log is more of a stage, really. That's because, at any moment, from the darkness will emerge a person, a storyteller, to sit upon that log, for a few minutes, and share a spooky tale. The person could be anyone from any spot on earth. You don't know exactly what to expect next, but you do know this: each person's story is claimed to be true. And it's usually something he or she experienced first-hand. Perhaps it will be a ghost story, or an alien encounter, or a monster attack, or an angel, a demon, or something too strange to even fathom. It could be almost anything.

That scenario is precisely what you hold before you. It may be impossible to experience that enchanted evening physically, but the magic of technology has made it possible on paper. Thanks to the power of media and the Internet, people from all over the world have come forth to share a personal experience. And those hair-raising testimonies are in this little book.

I have been collecting strange stories for more than 20 years. I began on a local scale, working in the Blue Ridge Mountains of western North Carolina, where I was born. As a teenager, I spread posters and ads around my town, Asheville, requesting weird, true stories. I was amazed when my mailbox was flooded with tales of fairy folk, flying saucers, disembodied spirits, and inter-dimensional time warps. Those stories were compiled in a book called *Speaking of Strange*. And, as years passed, I wondered when the time would be ripe to expand the project. I continued publishing and building a global audience through television and radio work. I recently realized it was finally the perfect time to present my invitation to the entire world. And I was delighted to see the stories flood in once again. Nothing had changed.

I only asked for these personal experiences to be true, short, and creepy. It didn't matter whether or not the submitter was a good writer or speller. I explained that editing would resolve any lack in writing prowess, and that slight embellishment could be provided to flesh out descriptive details. And it is important to note that I did not define "creepy." I did, however, provide the following true story as an example:

In 2002, in northern Connecticut, a 34-year-old brunette, named Jennifer Styles, found herself in a chilling position. I'm a well-known "ghost hunter," so she called me after a night of paralyzing fear. Jennifer had recently gone through a bad breakup and was searching for a new place to live. She worked at a law firm, and when a coworker named Toby heard of her situation, he suggested she rent a house he had recently inherited. It was a 3-story farmhouse in the countryside.

"Why don't you live there?" she inquired.

"Because it's haunted!" he said. The one night he tried to sleep there, he kept hearing footsteps on the long staircase. Jennifer had no fear and quickly took the amazing deal he offered.

The first night, all was well. Jennifer slept in the big bed on the third floor. There was nothing spooky, but at exactly 2 a.m., she shot up in bed, suddenly wide awake. After a few minutes, she went back to sleep. The second night, the exact same thing happened at 2 a.m. Upon hearing of this, Toby became curious. He loaned her a video camera and suggested she set it up while she sleep. The third night, as video was rolling, the same event occurred. She shot up at 2 a.m., then went back to sleep.

The next day, after returning from work, Jennifer rewound the video and watched it. The footage was stunning. In the green night shot, you can see her relaxed, slumbering away. Then at 1:58 a.m., a tall, dark, hooded figure appears to the left of the frame, and silently glides up to her bedside. It leans over her, like the grim reaper, as she sleeps. It quietly watches her until 1:59 a.m., and then glides away. At 2 a.m., Jennifer, wide and wild-eyed, shoots up in bed. Who are these phantoms? And why do they watch us when we sleep?

When someone submitted a story for this book, I gave that person the option of selecting a general category: Ghostly/Haunting, UFO/Alien, Cryptid/Interdimensional, ESP/Psychic, Spiritual, Synchronicity, or Other. The accounts sent in spanned the entire spectrum. I could have broken this book down into sections, by category. However, I find it far more interesting to mix them all up and allow you, the reader, to simply envision each story unfold without a particular expectation. You may not know what kind of story you're reading until you reach the very end. But that's part of the fun. It also happens to be a more realistic way of grasping these tales. You must remember that the person experiencing the phenomenon generally did not know, at the time, what was happening! That element is a crucial component in what makes these stories truly creepy. Put yourself in the author's place, often very confused as events were unfolding. Only in retrospect did the developing pieces seem to clarify.

Granted, we have no way of verifying that each of the stories is indeed true. I asked for true stories, and the teller of each professes it is true. We have the person's legal name and contact information, so we can at least say a real individual is willing to stand by the account's authenticity. So what more is there? Prior to cameras, wasn't all of history recorded this way, by human testimony? And it's important to consider how integral the human experience is to each of the stories. After all, we decide what is normal and what is paranormal, based on our level of understanding.

These stories are certainly entertaining. And yet, I believe they document something even more significant. Experiencing the unknown is what humbles us and reminds us of our place in this gigantic universe. There's something very creepy about simply acknowledging how small we look compared to the infinite blackness of space all around us. What is out there? And perhaps, more importantly, what is right...*here*...with us?

Welcome to the campfire.

THE FUNERAL OF FLOWERS

Jennifer Donnelly

Security Officer

Denver, Colorado, 1996

My sister and I would often play on a trail behind our parents' apartment complex. My favorite time of the year to visit this area had been in spring, just after the chill of winter left and the ice melted, which gave us a creek we could splash around in. There were blooming trees to climb and lilac bushes by the dozen to stick our noses in and inhale the lovely aroma. It was while our noses were buried deeply into one and our hands filled with lilac sprigs to take home to Mom, that an elderly woman appeared behind us. We were startled at first, but she had such a warm smile and wrinkly face, we soon realized we had nothing to fear and smiled back at her.

"Lilacs, just lovely, aren't they?" she asked us, bustling in between us to smell them herself. "They're my favorite flower; they just smell so good." She took in another lungful then pulled back to look at my sister and me, her face suddenly filled with sadness. "I can remember them at Lincoln's funeral. The smell of them, so strong, so sad, but they still remain my favorite."

"President Lincoln?" I asked and she nodded.

"It was a grand funeral. Do you remember it?" I shook my head and glanced at my sister, who returned my look with just as much bemusement. Lincoln had been buried in 1865, as we had learned in school. We were in the year 1996—131 years after Lincoln had been buried; of course we couldn't remember it. Not to mention, we were in the heart of Denver, hundreds of miles away from Lincoln's grave. I turned around, wishing to ask the lady more questions, but found she had vanished. There was no sign of her anywhere.

We never spoke about her again, the incident fading from my sister's memory (she had been seven years old at the time, and when I asked her if she remembered that lady a few years ago, she could not recall the meeting), but has since remained strong in my mind. It wasn't until a few weeks ago when I was reminded again of the lady. I saw a lilac bush while listening to an audiobook of *Abraham Lincoln, Vampire Hunter*, and I wondered if lilacs were even at his funeral. I immediately did a Web search and found that his funeral was known as the "funeral of flowers"; soldiers threw lilacs on the street in front of his carriage, the blooms being crushed, releasing the scent and forever jading those in attendance's memories at the smell. The realization that I had met a lady who claimed to be there had me anxious, in near tears, and even now as I write the words down, has my skin prickling.

THE BUTCHER KNIFE AND THE BATHTUB

Thomas Glenn Kelly

Wholesaler

Minneapolis, Minnesota, 1997

In 1997, my girlfriend and I were renting a huge, beautiful, old duplex in south Minneapolis. My girlfriend worked the night shift, 10:00 p.m. to 7:00 a.m. I would go to bed just after she left for work and she would wake me in the morning when she returned home.

One morning she woke me up and asked me why there was a butcher knife in the bathtub. I told her I had no idea, and we laughed it off. A few weeks later, she woke me up and asked why the bone-cutters were in the bathtub. Again we laughed it off, as the kitchen was adjacent to the bathroom and the butcher-block knife holder was on the counter just outside the bathroom.

A month or so later a similar thing happened; my girlfriend asked why the bone-cutters were in the bathroom sink. This odd occurrence continued throughout the three years we lived in the duplex. A total of probably 10 times, somehow in the night, kitchen cutlery ended up in the bathtub or the bathroom sink—once in the toilet. Toward the end of our time there, twice, the butcher knife was laying at the foot of our bed.

During our last weekend in the duplex, we threw a party and invited the downstairs tenants. They were a couple who had lived in the building for years and during the course of conversation and drinks, the subject of our landlord came up. We both went white when they informed us that in 1968, our landlord's mother had committed suicide in our unit. In the bathtub. With a butcher knife.

I COULD HEAR IT BREATHING

Joseph R. Keever

Driver

Great Bend, Kansas, 1986

I lived upstairs in a three-room apartment, and my mom and dad were visiting from Illinois. They slept in my queen-size bed; I slept on a rollaway bed in my living room/bedroom, with my bed 3 feet away from the foot of theirs. One night, I was lying on my back when I heard someone walking up the stairs. I assumed it was my neighbor coming home, but then I heard my door opening. There was no way this could have happened as I always lock my door. I heard someone walking through the kitchen, but I could not move. I tried to sit up and tell Dad or Mom that someone was in the apartment, but I could not speak. I felt something touch my ankles. I really wanted to move or scream, but couldn't. I felt something moving up my legs then on to my chest, and I could hear it breathing and feel it breathe on my face. I was still unable to move. It growled in my face. Suddenly it was gone. I sat straight up, horrified at what just happened. To this very day I always sleep on my side, never on my back.

DO BAD DREAMS DO THIS?

Tracy

Entrepreneur

Garden City, Michigan, 1972

One night many years ago, I went to sleep and a few hours later I was awakened by the sound of gnashing of teeth and growling of what I thought was a very angry dog. I could feel its claws scratching into my chest. I immediately started flailing at it to get it off of me, then jumped out of bed and ran to my parents' room. I knocked on their door. My mother opened it, and I told her what just happened. We went into my room, she looked around, including under my bed and proceeded to tell me it was just a bad dream. I pulled up my pajama top and showed my mom my chest. I asked her, "Do bad dreams do this?" My chest was covered with red claw marks!

THE CRASH

Barbara J. McNey

Retired Engineering Administrator

Cupertino, California, 1972

One morning at 4:30 a.m., I dreamed that the guy I was dating was in a terrible plane crash. In the dream, he was killed. My mom and sister came to break the news to me, and I was crying. I awoke from the dream very anxious and depressed as he was actually on a business trip in New York. Later that day I called him, but before I could say anything he said, "I'm glad you called; I was just getting ready to call you." He proceeded to tell me he had flown to Pennsylvania that morning and had been in a plane crash. He had been sitting next to the wing and it had caught on fire. As the plane went down, he was holding onto his rosary beads and thinking about me. The pilot landed safely in a field, and no one was seriously injured. This accident happened at precisely 7:30 a.m. and there is a 3-hour time difference between California and the East Coast; this means I dreamed about my boyfriend and the crash just as he was experiencing it!

THE PHANTOM PHOTOGRAPHER

Chase Wesley Jensen

Student

Montrose, Colorado, 2011

I bought a Kodak digital camera from Wal-Mart and was unhappy with the clicking sound that I heard coming from it when I first went to use it. I decided to return the camera and chose a new one of the same brand from the same store. When I returned home, I inserted batteries and proceeded to turn it on. I couldn't believe what I saw, as there in front of my eyes was a photograph of myself from the neck down already in the camera! I knew it was me as I was wearing the same shirt as in the photo! There was no way a store employee could have taken this photo as the camera was never removed from the box until I got home. Additionally, I couldn't have taken the photo of myself by accident as the perspective was from a distance, and I couldn't have taken such a photo on my own. I hadn't adjusted any of the settings so there was no way I had inadvertently turned on the self-timer. I was so amazed that I told my mom, and she couldn't believe it either. It was definitely one of the creepiest things I've ever encountered.

HOLLYWOOD HOBO

Corliss Sinclair

CNA in a Healthcare Center

Los Angeles, California, 1984

In 1984, I moved to Hollywood from Connecticut with my boyfriend Glen. We lived in North Hollywood, and being very close to Hollywood, we would often walk into town. One afternoon we were heading toward Vine Street and passed many recessed store fronts as we went. The construction of all these store fronts was similar: a tiled front floor with the door to enter, recessed way in, with display windows on each side. As we passed one business, I noticed a tall, dark-skinned man leaning inside the entryway. He was facing out and looking down the street toward us as we came walking up to Vine Street. I looked directly into his face and noticed his appearance. He was dressed in rumpled clothing, was unshaven with a slight beard, had long hair, and was very tall. Underneath all of that hobo clothing was a nice looking young man around 30 years old. He had a serious gaze as he returned my glance. We walked up a few more recessed doorways and there he was again—the same young hobo man! I found it rather startling, but I said nothing to Glen about it. We walked up and passed many more recessed businesses, and in yet another doorway, in the same position, there he was again! Each time our eyes met. It was the same man with the same serious gaze. By the third time, my own gaze became a stare.

That was it, I didn't see him again. I know he couldn't have run up past us as the sidewalks were very busy with pedestrian traffic and I would have seen him. Why did he show himself to me? Did he want to spook some young woman he didn't know? To this day, I do not understand how this could have happened, and I wonder if I had simply been looking at a ghost with nothing better to do on a Sunday afternoon.

THE SEGMENT IN THE SKY

William B. Francis

Systems Engineer, Optical Recognition

Deerfield, Tennessee, 1998

I was out on the front lawn around twilight. I was looking just above the barely visible tree line and toward southeast. At that time, I saw a brilliant, green, rectangular bar appear in the sky. At first I thought it was a green laser, but the amount of power that would have been required to have it appear as it did was huge. I held my arm out and attempted to gauge size and perspective; the bar was about two-fingers-wide at arm's length, and it appeared very sharp on all sides. I felt a crackling sound in the air. The whole episode lasted approximately 30 seconds. If it wasn't a laser that created the segment in the sky, where could that shaft of green light have come from? It was one of the truly vivid unexplained experiences I've had in my life.

IT WASN'T UFOS THAT SCARED HIM

Nita Anderson Hiltner

Retired Newspaper Reporter

Yucca Valley, California, Late 1970s

My sister and brother-in-law moved to Yucca Valley in the late 1970s. The area was known for UFO sightings and was a place people swore UFOs landed all the time, but it wasn't UFOs that scared my brother-in-law one night while he worked as a meter reader.

It was dark, and my brother-in-law, Chris, was driving down Old Woman Springs Road. Previously, late one night, my sister had seen an old woman walk through their living room into a wall, in a house on the same road. Chris was on his way home in the company truck when he saw a white mist forming ahead. He drove closer to the mist, and it enveloped the truck. Then it faded away except for his side of the truck. He looked to his left and through the window and saw the ghostly face of an old woman. He screamed and stepped on the gas and drove as fast as he could. The thing stayed with the truck no matter how fast he drove, so he stopped and jumped out of the truck. There was nothing around. He got home and told my sister to never tell anyone about his experience, as he was scared and people would think him crazy.

Fast forward a couple months. Chris and my sister had friends over to their house one day and the friends departed after dark. A half hour later, they got a phone call from them saying they had experienced the apparition themselves!

HER LAST GIFT

Mary Hominuk

Crisis Worker

Winnipeg, Manitoba, Canada, 1999

In 1993, my older sister committed suicide. A few years before her death, she had given me a tiny birthstone ring for my birthday. I greatly cherished this ring and was heartbroken when I lost it during a move. It was one of the last gifts she had given me and I searched everywhere for it. I truly mourned the loss of that ring.

The years passed, and I moved once more into the home I live in now. In 1999, my husband, son, and I were walking to the car, which was parked in front of the house. Something glittery on the lawn caught my eye. I reached down and picked up a dirt caked ring...the very birthstone ring I had lost years ago.

My sister gave me one more gift.

ROAD RUSH

Gary Chunn

Pest Control

Pontotoc, Mississippi, 1987

Leighton, David, and myself were returning home one night. We were all 17 years old, and had just dropped twin sisters off at home in Pontotoc, Mississippi near the Pontotoc and Lee county line just outside of Tupelo. David and I were dating the twins and Leighton was always the third wheel on these double-plus-one dates. We drank a lot back then, but not this particular night, as we had been with the twins and their dad would have killed us!

We dropped the twins off by their 11:00 p.m. curfew that night, then headed back to my house. We took a back road that we traveled all the time that was just a couple of miles from where I lived. One of the guys asked me to stop on the road so that he could relieve himself, and the other agreed that he needed to do the same. The road was gravel-topped and was lined with trees and fences on both sides.

When I stopped the car, it appeared as if the car was suspended off the road just a tad. It seemed as if the road kept passing underneath us, and I could see the trees, grass, and fence posts passing by equivalently on each side of the car. It appeared as if I was still driving on the road at about 30 miles per hour, which is the normal driving speed on this road. I knew the car was really stopped because I had the brake all the way down to the floor and was no longer guiding the wheel.

When my friends asked me why I wasn't stopping, I knew they were seeing the same thing. I told them that I had stopped the car. To prove it, I turned on the car's interior light and showed them that I was standing on the brake and not holding the steering wheel. David, Leighton, and I were so frightened I lifted my foot from the break, and this time floored the gas. About a quarter mile down the road, we bravely stopped to see if the same thing would happen again. It did not. I turned the car around and went back to the original spot, and the same thing happened exactly as it had before! Frightened again, I took off very fast and went home.

The experience was much like being dizzy, but instead of things twisting around us, they rushed past and underneath us. Inside the car, everything seemed very normal, just as everything had been a normal weekend night for us up to that point.

I often wonder if we had stayed to see what might have happened next, if we might have been carried into another dimension.

Throughout the years, we all have gone back to the same spot several times just to see if this would happen again, and it never has.

NO 25TH BIRTHDAY

Barbara J. McNey

Retired Engineering Administrator

Prescott, Arizona, 1972

In high school, I had a crush on a guy in my neighborhood named Gary. He told me that he "knew" somehow that he would die before his 25th birthday. I told him he was crazy. He went to Vietnam and came back safely. I said, "See! Your prediction didn't come true." He still insisted that he knew he would die before his 25th birthday.

Meanwhile, I moved out of state and we lost touch, but one day several years later, my mom called to tell me Gary had died in a construction accident. It was two weeks before his 25th birthday!

ENERGY BEING

Reba Duncan

Retired

Mira Loma, California, 1992

It was my first night in our new home alone. I was writing in the living room and my pen ran out of ink. I turned on the hall light, went down the hall to the bedroom, got a pen, and returned to the living room. I realized I needed more paper so I immediately went back to my bedroom, only this time, I did not turn any lights on.

Upon reaching the doorway to my room, I saw what I now describe as an "Energy Being" standing just outside my bathroom next to the sliding doors that went outside. He had his arms held high toward the sky as if basking in the energy from the moon. The Energy Being seemed to be deriving pleasure, moving its head side to side and smiling until it detected my presence. It held its head to one side, as if it were listening, then began to slowly back into my bathroom.

I was unable to see its features clearly, but could determine it was a male. The outline of its body was lit up like lights. It was almost cartoon-like. I ran back to the living room area where I slept for a long time thereafter.

STEPHEN

Jeannie Champine

Artist

Kewaunee, Wisconsin, 1991

During the early winter months along the shores of Lake Michigan, my friends and I ventured out to a historic hotel to have dinner. Much of the hotel was closed for the winter season, so only the bar and dining room areas were open that night.

Following dinner, we all headed to the bar area. Despite the cold outside, things inside were noisy and excited because the Packers were winning that night. I left the lively scene to use the restroom, and on my way back, decided to have a look around the rest of the beautiful Victorian-era hotel.

It had tall windows facing the lake that had just enough moonlight coming in through them so that I could see around the room. There were small tables and chairs arranged in cozy groups opposite the check-in desk, with thick carpet that ran the length of the reception area. My attention was drawn ahead to the dark, wooden staircase that led to the second floor. Looking back toward the bar area to make sure no one had noticed me missing, I ventured up the stairs. Upon reaching the first landing, I could make out rows of metal bed frames that lined both sides of the area, the mattresses rolled up for winter storage.

Just as I was thinking that I should get back to the bar, I noticed a light on around the corner at the far end of the landing area. I wondered why anyone would be up on this level and decided to investigate. The floor creaked under my feet as I tried to quietly maneuver to the light. I paused to make sure I didn't hear anyone coming to look for me. I rounded the corner to discover four steps leading to a beautiful, heavy, wooden door. I stood there amazed, staring at the craftsmanship and construction. There was thick dust layered on the steps, and clearly visible in the dust were small footprints; a lone child had recently been through this door. I hadn't seen any children in the hotel restaurant, and certainly there weren't any in the bar. I could only rationalize that the child was in some kind of trouble so I picked up my foot to climb the stairs. Before my foot touched the first step there was a very loud, startling noise as the heavy door exploded open! It slammed against the wall, and the coldest wind I have ever felt rushed over me like a raging, ice-cold river! I moved faster than I ever had before, in my rush to get back to the bar and the crowd of people there. I was pale and trembling as I collapsed onto a seat. I couldn't blink, speak, or think clearly. The bartender leaned down in front of me and asked what had happened.

"I don't know...I...I...I'm not sure. I...I can't...I didn't...I...." I continued stammering. When I looked into his eyes, I could see that he knew. He knew exactly what had happened to me. His face went white as his eyes grew round and opened wide as he said, "You met Stephen."

"Stephen? Who is Stephen?"

Casting glances to either side, the bartender leaned closer to my ear, "I just broke up with my girlfriend. I have been pretty bummed about it. Yesterday I was on my hands and knees polishing the fancy glassware, when I broke down. I started crying. I didn't want anyone to know, so I just stayed there on the floor. I felt someone rubbing my back telling me it was alright, and not to cry. I felt so much better...until I realized I was the only one in the hotel! The kitchen staff had gone into town to pick up food for dinner service! Things like this happen a lot. The rest of the staff are from this area and grew up with Stephen's story."

I asked what the story was, and the bartender continued, "One night, a couple arrived after dark with a little boy. They skipped out the next day without paying their bill. The manager went up to the room to see if they had left anything behind to pay what they had owed, only to find their little boy there. Dead. We decided to call him Stephen."

So, Stephen has never left the hotel.

IT SLITHERED INTO THE ROOM

Margaret Eyer

Retired

St. Louis, Missouri, 1966

In 1966, my parents bought an old Victorian home. My father was going through the house, making sure everything was in working order, and the last place to check was the attic. The attic was accessed through a secret door in an upstairs bedroom closet. While in the attic, he found it to be musty and hot. Upon crawling further, he suddenly felt an ice cold chill, and startlingly, his head was pushed into the wall! After leaving the attic, and without saying anything for several months, other members of the family experienced other paranormal activities.

One evening, my parents were having their own problem with the ghost. It called out my mother's name, for her to come to the top of the stairway. Dad told her not to go. After calling her a second time, the spirit returned to the room and shook the bed violently. It was a long night for our family. Who knows what would have happened to my mother if she had gone to the top of the stairs.

Later that same night, through the slightly ajar door of the room my older sister and I shared, there flowed a bluish-gray mist. It slithered into the room and across the ceiling toward my sister. I watched in horror until I couldn't stand it anymore, finally pulling the sheet up over my head, unable to sleep the rest of the night. I laid there petrified, afraid that if I removed the sheet and came face-to-face with it, I would die of fright.

IT WAS SATAN

David McCoy

Technician

Eight Mile, Alabama, 1973

The year was 1973 on the campus of Mobile College (now known as the University of Mobile). This college was a Baptist liberal arts college, and most of the men that lived on campus were ministerial students. The men's dormitory had been converted into an additional women's dormitory, and the men now had "cottages" that were designed with two bedrooms that shared a living room and bath. This was the first semester that my good friend Johnny (a ministerial student) and I had attended this college, and we were roommates. The atmosphere was always peaceful, until one night....

I usually slept on my stomach facing my closet, which was in the opposite direction from Johnny's bed. Johnny had gone to bed at about 10:30 that evening, but I stayed up until 11:30 studying for a test. Around 1:30

a.m., while in a very sound sleep, I was awakened by a blood curdling scream from Johnny. He screamed three times and I was paralyzed with fright, unable to move. After the screams he continued to moan.

I slid off my bed, onto my hands and knees. I crawled to my closet, feeling around inside for my robe. I wrapped it around me and made my way into the living room and stood against the table shaking like a leaf, when Johnny came slowly into the room. I yelled at him, "What did you do that for?!"

Though Johnny was a big guy, he weakly said, "I don't know. I was lying in my bed and I saw this white form float into the room and it hovered over me. I tried to scream, but the sound wouldn't come out of my mouth. I shut my eyes and when I opened them back up, it was still hovering over me, but somehow my head was at the foot of the bed. I tried to scream again but nothing came out. I closed my eyes and when I opened them again, the white form was gone, and I was lying back in my bed correctly."

I explained to him that this same thing had happened to some other male students a few years prior to our incident. They said it had been Satan or one of his demons that was responsible for the terror. It had come in through a window in the old dorm building and hovered over two different students who were in their beds. They too had been horrified and had a large prayer meeting in the middle of the night. Several students had been "saved" thanks to that incident.

A moment after I had said the name "Satan," it sunk into my big, strong friend Johnny's head. He started crying like a baby, and he screamed hysterically, "That's what it was! It was Satan! It was Satan!" No one slept the rest of that night. It was a really big deal the next day on campus.

A HUSBAND'S COMFORT

Brenda Kilpatrick Bates

Retired

Glenville, North Carolina, 2011

My husband was killed when a tree fell on him. His back was turned, and I don't think he saw it coming. During the following months of grief, I had many dreams of him that mostly left me confused. One night I dreamed of him and decided not to be upset, but instead confront him and ask him about his sudden death. In the dream, we were in a paneled room with books and chairs. I asked him about his death. He proceeded to sit down in one of the chairs, get up, move to another chair, and sit down. Then he said, "It was like knowing you sat in that chair, but finding yourself in this chair." My question was answered; I don't think he felt a thing.

THE PORCELAIN GIRL

Bill Fischbach

Factory Worker

Unknown Location and Year

Everyone has their own ideas and beliefs regarding the existence of ghosts. I personally have had enough personal experiences with them that I believe they exist.

When I was young, I awoke one night and saw a very short, curly-headed girl sitting at the edge of my bed. She was so little that her feet didn't touch the floor, and she just kicked her legs back and forth in the air. She had a very pale, porcelain-like complexion, and she was dressed in bright, white clothing. All around her there seemed to be a bright glowing light which encompassed her presence. She was just sitting there looking around the room, when all of a sudden, she saw that I was awake and looking at her. She appeared startled, and she quickly disappeared.

I'm not sure to this day if she was a ghost or perhaps my very own guardian angel, but I am 100-percent sure that she was really there.

EYES ON THE SKIES

Kelly Colby

Wellness Researcher

DFW Airport, Texas, 2011

I was in the middle of a really bad time in my life. I was dealing with the after-effects of the death of my still-born daughter and a host of personal health problems. My relationship was at the end of its road, and there was a lot of pain in my life. I was living in Guatemala but was back and forth to Dallas, because I made my money in the United States.

I was in Dallas staying in an extended-stay hotel. The hotel literally backed up to the airport and there was a small pond at the back of the hotel. I went out one night and laid on the ground to just calm down and clear my head. I loved watching the airplanes fly overhead. Because it was night, flights had ceased for the evening, so everything was peaceful and quiet except for the night sounds and the highway off in the background.

As I lay watching the stars, suddenly, the feeling of the night changed. All of the sounds of insects stopped and I could no longer hear any cars or background noise whatsoever. Everything fell into an eerie silence. This is when I saw something that was triangular-shaped come across the sky in very slow motion. It was not far above me, but it was completely silent. The strange thing did not block out the night sky, as it was almost transparent except for the edges. I could barely make out the outline. It moved slowly toward the airport but disappeared to me because I could no longer make out the edges. I am farsighted, so it had to be close enough that I could make out the outline and it was massive but not so extraordinarily massive that I could not see the outer edges. If it flew away or went somewhere else, I'll never know.

I laid there for awhile certain of what I had seen, but telling myself I was crazy. When I came to my senses again, everything around me was normal; the sounds of the night returned and it no longer felt strange or creepy, except that I personally felt a little freaked out and creepy. I went in and told my husband. Luckily he believed me, despite the condition of our relationship.

I haven't seen anything like it before nor have I told anyone about it before now. I have often wondered if the trauma of my situation simply made me sensitive to perceiving whatever it was.

ALWAYS DURING A SNOWSTORM

James Eric Freeman

Mechanical Engineer

Salt Pond Road in Troutville, Virginia, December 2010

We moved from the city out into the country when my son was just about to start high school. Several odd things had happened during the first few years, including odd noises, devices inexplicably turning on in the middle of the night, knocks, and bumps. None of the phenomena seemed ominous or particularly menacing, so I wasn't bothered by the occurrences; I was intrigued. My wife and son didn't feel the same way, as they had several personal encounters that were unexplained and not quite as "friendly." Through the years, we had noticed something common amongst all occurrences: they always seemed to happen during a snowstorm. In addition, it seemed that most of the things that happened were tied to an upstairs bedroom that we used as a spare bedroom and office. It was the epicenter.

On December 18, my wife Stacy, son Gage, and myself were home at about four in the evening. A major snowstorm was heading our way, and I had a load of wood on the front deck that needed to be brought in and stacked on the hearth. Flurries had already begun, and the wood for the fireplace was getting a slight dusting. Gage got dressed, put on a hoodie, and began bringing in wood. Stacy was in the kitchen baking Christmas cookies, and I was in the computer room lacing up my boots to go help with the wood. The storm was ramping up fast, and we were burning daylight. From my vantage point in the office, I could see most of the house, including the suspended walkway that adjoined the second floor bedrooms to the rest of the house.

As I finished lacing my boots, I heard Gage come in again, and when I glanced up, I saw him walking slowly across the upstairs walkway toward the bedrooms. His hood was up on his black jacket, and his hands were in his pockets. "Ahh, gloves!" I thought. He must be getting them from his bedroom before bringing in more snow-covered wood. I looked back down, grabbed my jacket, and headed to the door to the deck to start helping. As I reached for the door, it opened into my hand. Gage came walking in saying, "Well, this is about the last of it." He had his arms full of wood, wearing no gloves, and his red hoodie was pulled up over his head, dusted with pure-white snow.

Many things went on that evening, including discussions about selling the house and moving away. Cooler heads prevailed and we stayed. All has been calm since. As an odd side note, our small black lab Lilly disappeared that day, and we have never seen her since.

•••••

As I typed the story I just submitted about the black, hooded figure, my wife was downstairs. Near completion, I heard the front door slam loudly. Just as I submitted the story, my wife came upstairs and said she was in the kitchen when she heard the slam. She went to the front door and it was slightly ajar, as if it had been slammed hard and cracked back open slightly. This door is rarely used and the deadbolt and regular lock are always engaged. She went out on the deck to investigate, and there was nothing in any direction, all the way to the tree line. Coming up the steps to tell me what happened, she also noticed the guest room door (now a nursery) was closed. We always leave it open.

Perhaps relocation is not a bad idea after all.

VACATION CHILL

Ex-Navy Nuke

Engineer

Savannah, Georgia, 2006

My wife and I went to Savannah, Georgia, for a mini-vacation near the end of summer a few years ago. While there, we stayed at a popular hotel chain directly on the Savannah River. We arrived on Thursday and some Navy friends of ours came down from Virginia to spend some time with us. We had a marvelous time seeing the sites in Savannah and hearing about the yellow fever outbreak in the early colonial days which killed quite a few of the settlers. Of course, we heard many ghost stories while on our tours about the buildings in Savannah.

It was Saturday night, and our friends decided to leave a bit early to visit family in central Georgia, so my wife and I decided to go to bed early that night. We packed our bags and placed them neatly against the wall in preparation for a quick getaway in the morning.

Everything was peaceful until 3:12 a.m., when I was startled awake for some reason. When I awoke, I noticed the bags that were so neatly placed against the wall were now strewn about as if someone was looking for something. I assumed that my wife had been up during the night and had been looking for something and had left the bags unorganized. I got up and neatly rearranged the bags and laid down to go back to sleep.

Just as my head touched the pillow and I pulled up the covers, the coldest hand I had ever felt in my life ran its fingers through my hair! I have worked in Minnesota with -60 degree temperatures, and the hand that ran through my hair felt colder than that! I immediately looked over at my wife, thinking it had to be her. As I reached out and looked over at her, her back was facing me and she was completely out of my reach! Who the hell had touched me?!

Feeling a bit exasperated, I jumped out of bed and looked around the room (without my glasses), and could not see anything odd. I was definitely awake, so I decided to turn on the light near the desk in the room and surf the Internet until my wife awoke. I was continuously looking over my shoulder for anyone or anything else that might sneak up on me again.

My wife awoke around 4:00 a.m., came over and gave me a kiss, and then went in to take her shower. When she finished I told her that it was time to leave and that I thought I'd had a ghostly experience that night. She immediately responded with, "Well that would explain what happened to me the night before last!" She proceeded to tell me that she was mysteriously awoken at 3:12 a.m. (I hadn't told her the time of my occurrence yet), and when she woke she looked toward the bathroom and noticed the outline of a man. My wife, fearing no man (her daddy was an army drill sergeant), jumped out of bed and proceeded to chase the unknown perpetrator into the bathroom. However, when she opened the bathroom door, no one was to be found! She dismissed it at the time as a dream, though she would have sworn that she had been wide awake during the incident. After I had told her my story she said to me, "It's time to leave!" which at this point, I could not and would not argue with!

The hotel just happened to have red velvet wallpaper in the hallways, and while I was walking to the elevator, I couldn't help imagining a scene from *The Shining*. All I could see was the boy riding his three-wheeler down the hallways, then turning a corner and seeing the two dead girls at the end of the hallway! My imagination was running wild, and I had no such occurrence. On the way out of the hotel, I told the night clerk what had happened. She locked us out of the hotel with some of our bags still inside, so we had to wait until a man came out to smoke, before we were able to retrieve our remaining bags!

WHAT ARE THE CHANCES?

Steven R. Thomas

Inventory

Antioch, California, 1977

I was 19 years old and worked for a manufacturing company that offered two weeks of paid vacation as a perk. I decided to spend the first week with my grandparents, who lived 457 miles north from me, and the second week at home.

I took a bus to my grandparents' house in Antioch, California. My grandfather and I loved to go fishing together, so he had set up a variety of fishing trips for us. Each morning, we would get up around 3:00 or 4:00 to prepare for that day of fishing.

On Friday morning, we were loading the boat, and I noticed a familiar van driving down my grandfather's street. As the van came closer, I could see who was driving it, so I stopped the van with a wave. The driver of the van was a coworker who worked next to me on the manufacturing line. I asked him what he was doing in the neighborhood, and he told me that he and a friend had spent the night on the beach in Pismo. They had gotten lost and were trying to get back onto the freeway. My grandfather does not live on a busy, major street. He had gotten lost and was turning around, and just happened to come down the street that I was on at 4:00 a.m.? It was very odd. I took a bus ride back home that Saturday afternoon, and my grandfather passed away just two days later.

MY JUICE

Benjamin Ramon Andrade

Xerox Machine Operator

Gardena, California, April 2013

My house is a little creepy, but we love it anyway. Our family somewhat turned our home into a hospice as we cared for two of my great-aunts. Both of these aunts passed away in our home due to old age and cancer. The house is what I would refer to as "a normal house," however we do hear odd noises. These strange sounds consist of bumps in the night, doors being slammed, and pots and pans and cabinet doors being slammed in the kitchen. Some people have even claimed to hear voices right before bedtime. So what does this have to do with my juice? Everything.

Every morning before my family leaves for school and work, my wife pours me a Mason jar of cran-cherry juice. Every morning, cran-cherry juice. One April morning around 9:00 a.m., my wife set out my drink before she and my child left the house. I saw my jar on the counter and it was full of juice. I said to myself,

"That juice is going to taste good when I drink it." I decided to complete a chore before enjoying my morning refreshment. I came back from the task, and the glass was empty; there was a mere quarter teaspoon of liquid in my twelve-ounce jar! The jar was not broken, so the beverage did not leak out, and I was home alone, so no other human drank it. I decided to pour myself a new glass to see if I could trigger the effect again. I considered the possibility that I may have drank the juice and had simply forgotten. I decided I definitely did not drink it. So who or what did?

WHAT IF I HAD TOUCHED IT?

Mary Jane Collins

Nashville, Tennessee, 2002–2003

After waking one night and being awake for a few moments—stretching, yawning, and preparing to go back to sleep—I noticed a slowly swirling mass of energy in the room with me. I rubbed my eyes and looked again, and it started to come together in the form of a vertically-oriented, swirling, galaxy shape, with what resembled a black hole at the center. I rubbed my eyes again and it was still there, very interesting to look at!

It looked as if it had iridescent clear colors overlaid on the room's background. You could see right through it like a heat mirage on a hot road in the summertime.

Intrigued by it, I got up and walked over to it to get a closer look. I wanted to touch it, or stick my head inside and have a look. Then a quick fear came over me that if I did, I may not come back after what would seem like being sucked in with the force akin to an airline toilet flush. I stood and looked at it for a while and decided that was enough, and did nothing to break the apparent plane of energy.

I laid back down and watched it for a little while longer; it slowly faded away. I haven't seen it since. I still wonder what it was and what would have happened if I hadn't become afraid of the unknown. What if I had touched it or stuck my head in the center to have a look see? It was fascinating and a little creepy, all at the same time.

ONE LAST LOOK

Julieann E. Peters

Chula Vista, California, 1987

I bought my little mobile home from an elderly woman who was moving to Oregon to live with her son's family. Her sister used to live across from her and had died. One evening, about two years after I moved in, I was alone watching television on the couch when from the corner of my eye, I thought I saw someone walk in my bedroom. My bedroom was all the way down the hallway to my left. I turned my head to get a better look at what I had seen and nothing was there. It happened again a few minutes later, so I got up and checked my bedroom and no one was there.

About half an hour later, off to the left of the television, I thought I saw someone slowly walk in front of the big mirror that was on the wall. By this time I was wondering what was going on, but for some reason I wasn't scared.

The next day I couldn't wait to tell a coworker about what had happened. She was Hawaiian and was into strange phenomena. She thought I had had a spirit visit, but I couldn't imagine who it would have been. The next day I was watering my yard and the elderly lady who lived behind me came out to chat. She told me that Vera, the lady I bought the trailer from, had died two days prior. I told her about what I experienced the night before and how I wondered if it was Vera that I had seen. She went on to tell me that her son said that Vera regretted moving and really missed her little trailer. I guess Vera wanted to take one last look before moving on. I have never seen her again.

NOSE DROPS...DADDY?

Charles Thomas Allen

Adelphi, Maryland, 1958

I am a 66-year-old man. When I was 10 years old, I called out to my father, in the middle of the night, with the words, "Dad, I need nose drops!" as I had a stuffy nose. In the 1950s, nasal decongestant sprays in squeeze bottles were not in use. As I did not hear my dad respond to my call, I called out again. At that moment, I noticed that my dad was standing at my bed side. Feeling relaxed to see him standing there in the moonlight within my room, I sat up in my bed to thank him for getting up to help me. Immediately, I realized that the silhouette shape of my dad was pitch black and completely silent. The figure of the man did not verbally reply to my statement of joy, but only appeared to lean toward me holding out a dropper in his right hand. For a moment, I looked closely at the "shadow man." I felt frightened, so I turned away from the black figure and pulled the bed covers over my head. Nothing happened, so after about 10 minutes had passed, I sheepishly peeked out from under the covers to see that the shadow man had gone. I did not call out again that night.

A MURDER OF CROWS

Melissa Briese

Home Organizer

Afton, Virginia, 2002

I moved in with a friend in Virginia, who was a single dad, to help him out with his finances and kids. It was not a smooth transition. I was abruptly woken up every night around 1:00 a.m. from a horrifying dream involving large, black birds swooping down at me. On the fourth night, I woke again from this reoccurring nightmare, only this time I saw a man who appeared to be from the 1800s sitting on my bed. He faded away, along with the imprint on the mattress where he had been sitting. I woke up my friend, who does hypnosis, and we went to work on getting me to tune into this dream and apparition, to find its meaning and resolution.

In the hypnosis session, I was talking as if I were the man from the 1800s. This man stated that he was dabbling in black magic when he was alive, using his will to gain power over others. One of his favorite tools was a murder of crows that would harass his enemies, scratching and biting them. This became his calling card. Unfortunately for him, he got sloppy in his practice and the tables turned. Through a dramatic series of events, the dark magician's own army of birds attacked him and pecked him to death. My friend counseled the misguided spirit and eventually got him "into the light." As this session was coming to a close, there was a loud bang at the front door. We finished, and we went to investigate the noise. There in the center of the front stoop, with its wings spread out majestically, was the largest black crow either of us had ever seen. It was dead.

BUBBA

Ernest E. Jonas Jr.

Dallas, Texas

My grandmother lived in San Antonio, Texas. She was in bed asleep around 10:00 p.m. when she abruptly awoke, sat up in bed, and blurted out loud my nickname, "Bubba!"

Four hundred miles away in Dallas, Texas, I was wide awake in my bedroom when I clearly heard her voice call out my nickname. My door was open, and the sound came from the hallway.

THE MIST

Missy Hill

Radio Host/UFO Sky Watch/Galactic Shamanism

Hobe Sound, Florida, 2000

My husband, Ron, and I were testing out our new RV at the Jonathan Dickinson State Park in Hobe Sound, Florida. It was a cool March evening in the year 2000, and we decided to go for a night hike. Our hike brought us near some railroad tracks, when all of a sudden we were engulfed by a thick, white mist which swirled about us languidly, chilling us both to our very bones. I turned to Ron and said, "I have this overwhelming feeling that someone, or maybe several people, were killed on these tracks." And right at that moment, while the dense, white mist continued to encircle us, a train went by, jarring Ron's memory. He said that during his first trucking job years ago, this old trucker told him a story about how, when he was a small boy back in the 1920s or 30s, an entire family had been obliterated by a train when their car inexplicably stalled on the tracks. The old trucker said he remembered the story vividly because his father was one of the poor men tasked with trying to find all the body parts strewn about the scene of the accident. As soon as Ron finished telling me the story, the mist dissipated, as if, in telling the story, the mist or spirits found release or validation.

A PARANORMAL LIFE

Omega

Groningen, Netherlands

My mom and I lived in a great home where many strange things would happen. When I was 9 years old, my mother said that she saw lights through the window at the back of the house. She went to investigate and when she opened the door, to her astonishment, she saw a massive spaceship hovering over the garden. She was very afraid and hurried back inside and closed the door. She told me about the incident a few days later, and I remembered the lights she was talking about. That same night, I had had a strange dream about an ambulance in the backyard. I had awoken from the dream thinking that it was impossible, as there was no way a vehicle could be in the backyard, which was way too small.

My mother had two businesses that she would have to close at the end of the day; sometimes it would be very late. One night, it was almost midnight, and I was home with my brother. I was reading my Donald Duck book in my bed which was a high sleeper with a desk under it. It was a red, iron bed with a ladder, and about five minutes after I settled in, I heard someone coming up the stairs. I heard three steps and I began to sit up in bed. I knew it was something strange, as I could feel it in my body and stomach. I tried to listen; I no longer heard anything, so I lay back and read my book again. Twenty seconds later, I heard the stairs again, it was coming up the stairs! I quickly covered myself under my blanket and put the book on my face. I heard the person at the top of the stairs and then I heard its footsteps as it came into my room. I was dying inside! It came into my room and climbed up onto my bed and sat next to my head. I was too afraid to open my eyes under the book; I could feel it sitting next to my head. I went into shock mode and was thinking many strange things. I did not know exactly how long I was lying there, but my mom was away for a few hours. I heard my mother's keys in the door and I jumped out of my high bed and I screamed. It was really the scariest thing ever!

Not long after that happened, I was lying in my bed in the same room, only now I shared it with my brother and we had gotten a bunk bed. My mother had just had my baby sister, but still went out to close our shops. After she left, I was lying in bed. My brother had fallen asleep first, and I was thinking about the day. It was very dark in our room, but I was not feeling afraid at that moment. After 10 minutes, I thought I saw something on the wall; it was a colored dot. It shined like very bright neon and then suddenly the dot multiplied! It multiplied itself into many, many dots that were all the same color and all in a perfect line. They changed neon colors, from blue to pink to green and even a color I had never seen before! I couldn't believe what I was seeing, and I became very scared. I tried to look away and I closed my eyes tightly. This was when I realized I could still see the dots with my eyes closed! That's when I really began to panic, because it seemed to be in my eyes. I tried to wake my brother by kicking the bunk bed above me, only he wouldn't wake up. I don't know what happened next as I passed out. When I woke up, it was as if nothing had happened.

When I was 11 years old, I had an out of body experience on three separate occasions, each while watching television. For this to have happened to a young child was a very scary thing. I was floating above myself in sitting position. I was able to turn things on with my mind, like my mobile and my radio.

I have seen UFOs everywhere. I have seen more than 50 through my life so far, and I feel some type of connection to them. I know that this is very strange to say, but it's what I feel. The closest one that I ever saw was next to my window when I was 9 years old, only one or two meters away.

With all of these different, strange things that have happened, I don't feel like I am an average person. I know I am very different, like I am from somewhere else. I think very differently and I can do things nobody can even imagine with my eyes, such as seeing things even with my eyes closed. I see things like people and figures and many other things all in vivid color, all day and every day. I am also very good at reading body language and can read people's minds in some strange way.

I dream about my future and almost all of the things that I dream happen later in my life. When I see that my dreams are coming true, it's like having déjà vu. At first I found it hard to believe, but after it happening so many times I can no longer say they are simple dreams. Sometimes it feels like I am in a movie. I know I am not crazy as I am a very smart person with a very good heart, and I would never lie to myself like that. I have many more stories to tell about what happened to me in life and still is happening.

I have always had many unexplained things happening to me, from when I was little until now—so many things, that I could never write them all down.

A GOLDEN HISTORY

Timothy D. Du Fore

Nevada City, California, 2003

The old northern California home where I was living for a few months had once been an old brothel in a former lively gold rush era town. It was also reportedly haunted. My roommates had filled me in on the reported encounters with ghostly apparitions. These included footsteps on the stairs, and strange sounds reminiscent of female laughter and whispers that would resound through the three-story house. This house was old and worn. When you entered, you felt a chill and an uneasy feeling, like the walls were watching you.

One weekend, my daughter came to visit me. I showed her through the house and began to explain to her that I thought the house was haunted. As we made our way to the rear of the house—the family room, as we called it—I suddenly jumped. Something that couldn't be seen had grabbed the back of my neck and put its fingers around me. It was icy and electric, and my hair stood on end.

My daughter who was in front of me opened the sliding glass door to go outside, and as she was in front of me, she went outside and the sliding glass door slowly closed itself when no one was near it. This door did not move freely and had to really be forced with two hands to close. It closed right before my eyes as the icy hand released its grip off the back of my neck. My daughter believed in ghosts after that, and I have never again visited that haunted abode.

A CRY FOR HELP

Charlie P. Reesor

Sales

Brandenburg, Kentucky, 1980

When I was a small child, my family was not very wealthy, so we stayed at my grandmother's to save money in order to move. I shared a king-sized bed with my mother and father, so needless to say, it was hard to sleep at times. I remember one night in particular; my mother and I were up late talking while my father snored loudly next to us. Out of nowhere, we both started hearing the faint sound of a woman's voice—she was trying to say something! We immediately stopped talking to listen more closely. The voice was approaching us, so Mom woke Dad up for him to hear. He said it was just a dog and to go back to sleep. As it got near the open window, we could hear it more clearly. It was saying, "Help me." My dad heard it, jumped up, and yelled at it! It left the house through the window, and whatever it was, you could hear it running through the tall weeds toward the cemetery!

The next day we went to put flowers on my grandfather's grave, and the ones that were previously there had been moved to a lady's grave who'd died in a tornado in 1974. Her name was Martha Sonn, and her kids were all taken by the tornado. My mother was friends of the Sonns.

There's no doubt in my mind that the voice we all heard was Martha Sonn's looking for her kids.

A SHOCKING STORM

Bobby Dulaney

Flooring

Selma, North Carolina, 1989/1990

I was born and raised in North Carolina, though I have since moved away. As a child, my father and mother were concerned about the storms, especially the tornados and hurricanes that would hit the area we lived in. We regularly would load up the car with my brother, mother, father, and myself, and head to the hospital to ride out a storm.

On this particular night at approximately 8:00 or 9:00 p.m., we all got in the car and decided to wait and see what happened with the weather before leaving. I was in the back on the passenger's side, Dad was driving with Mom beside him, and my brother was beside me. The lightning was really bad, as was the rain. I had a small pillow with me that I always brought along that was sitting on my lap. After about 10 minutes, I looked out my window up at the clouds, and in the split second it took the lightning to splinter across the sky, I saw 10 soldiers. Four were in the front kneeling, and four were standing behind them, flanked on each side with one more kneeling man. I immediately buried my face in the pillow on my lap and started hysterically sobbing and screaming. To this day, I've never seen anything like it and have only told four people of this until now.

CHRISTMAS AT GRANDMA'S

Joseph T. Hill

Legal

Canton, Ohio, 2000

We were having an annual gathering at my grandmother's home. She lived in an old two-story city house build around 1900. Growing up, the home always had an unexplainably creepy feel to it, so I never spent too much time there. On Christmas Eve, with family members numbering about 15 to 20, we sat in the living room circled around the Christmas tree. The tree was in a corner on a platform and stood about five feet tall. I noticed that the tree shook slightly a few times, and could tell others did too. Suddenly the tree rose, levitating about six inches in the air. It violently rotated 180 degrees and then simply sat back down. The room grew silent; everyone had witnessed it, and nobody knew what to think or say about it. Grandma seemed unfazed about what had just happened. She said that it had happened before and not to talk about it.

To this day, this occurrence is the strangest thing I have ever witnessed.

GIVE THEM BACK!

Ranetta Tyler

Lubbock, Texas, 2010-2013

I went out with my husband one night and wore my blue diamond earrings. After we got home, I took off my jewelry and set my earrings on the shelf behind me in the living room, thinking I would grab them in the morning before the kids got home. I ended up forgetting about them until I was going to put them on the next weekend. I went to look for them on the shelf and could not find them. I saw two little finger swipes and the marks in the dust where the earrings had been sitting. I immediately asked my 3-year-old son what he had done with them. He was adamant he had not touched them. I searched all over the house for them with a flashlight, looking in every crack or crevice they could have fallen into or been placed—to no avail. After a few weeks, I gave up.

About six weeks later, a friend was over and we were talking about our experiences with ghosts. She brought up my blue diamond earrings and what a shame it was they were lost. I said that I just wanted whoever took them to give them back! The next day my parents were over to take us out to dinner, and before we left, I went to put on perfume. There my earrings were, sitting on the shelf right next to my perfume bottle in plain daylight. I had looked there at least 10 times!

We lived in that house for three years (an old rock/quartz/petrified wood house built in the early 1940s) and had multiple odd things happen. My son began talking about odd things and described what he called "Mossums," beings that would come out of the sky and eat the lightning, along with several imaginary friends with whom he had very detailed relationships. Several times, things like a sippy cup or playing cards would fly off counters and shelves. Banging noises on the side of the house would be loud enough to make the house vibrate. I'd get scared and grab my pistol to go search for whatever was making the noise. Friends of ours pulled up to the house one night and saw a black shadow man standing beside the driver's side door of our Wagoneer. He looked up at them when they pulled up with their headlights on and walked off into the shadow of the house. The same friends saw a lady walking from our front door down the sidewalk on another occasion.

My husband and I have never fought so much as when we lived in that house. Previous owners of the property all ended up divorced. Apparently we got away in time.

THE ESCALATION OF TROUBLE

Sheena-Michelle

Fresno, California, 1992

I was 7 years old when my family moved into a home in Easton, south of the Fresno County area. My brothers and I shared a room where they had the bottom bunk bed and I had the top. I remember the first week in the house; I was sleeping, and the blanket was slowly pulled off of me. I pulled the blanket back up and over me, and never opened my eyes. The next night, the same thing happened, and I kept my eyes tightly shut again. The fourth night, I saw her. She was a tall woman in a bonnet, though she didn't look friendly. She approached my bed and, with a strong hand, yanked the blanket off of me! I jumped out of my bed and ran to my parents' room.

Gradually, whispering started to be heard in our pillows and other apparitions appeared to me. The spirits would mock our voices and take the form of us. It really got out of control. My mother was pregnant with my youngest brother when, one morning, she had been boiling water for tea. The entire pot, filled with boiling hot water, flew off of the stove, toward her pregnant belly. She was uninjured, though the intent was clear. That house was filled with bad vibes, demons, and ghosts.

HOME TIME

Vicky Knowlan

Andover, New Jersey, 1985

I lived in New Jersey, and they had raised the drinking age to 21. This meant that I had to travel to a bar on the New York State border on Saturdays to dance and watch bands play. I had a long, boring, hour and a half drive through northern New Jersey to get to my mom's house. I left the bar at exactly 1:30 a.m., sober, as I was afraid that if I drank I'd fall asleep behind the wheel. That particular night, I was tired even though I had gotten plenty of sleep the night before. I was 4 miles from my mom's house when I suddenly felt extraordinarily sleepy. I was afraid that if I pulled over in the zero-degree temperature, I would freeze to death. I kept telling myself that I just had to stay awake just a short while longer; the week before, my friend had fallen asleep behind the wheel of his truck leaving that very bar and totalled his truck, but luckily wasn't hurt.

As I made my way up a long hill, the windy road forked to the right. I could not believe how enormous the moon was; a plate held at arm's length in front of you would have been equivalent in size! I was staring and thinking, "It's gotta be the moon. I can see craters, but it's as if it's magnified 100 times!" Seeing this beautiful sight reinvigorated me. I wanted to pull over on the shoulder and stare at it, but I kept driving. At the top of the hill, the road bent 90 degrees to the left, and the topography dictated that there was a deep, wooded valley directly behind me. That's when I saw a light a couple of miles behind me that appeared to be weaving down a hill. However there was no hill behind me, nor was there a road! A bright spotlight shone in the back side window of my car, reflecting off of the back seat. I wondered if it was the moonlight as I glanced into the rearview mirror again and saw that the light was much closer. The single light had broken into two, so that they were travelling side-by-side. I wondered if it was two motorcycles, but despite my car being brand new, and there not being a radio, why couldn't I hear their engines? I should have heard them as they approached from behind me. I had been speeding, but the lights were able to catch up to me in minutes. The bright lights were now immediately behind me as I exclaimed, "What the hell!" That was the last thing I remember.

I was very awake, but I couldn't recall driving those last two miles to my mom's house. I found myself parked oddly at the bottom of her drive way, not at all where I usually parked. It should have been about 3:00 a.m., yet the sky looked slightly pink, as if the sun was rising. It was January, so it had to be closer to 7:00 a.m.! I was going to look at the clock to confirm the time, but all I could think of was how strange it was that I couldn't recall the last 2 miles of the drive, that I should really just go to bed.

It still bothers me that I had been so wide awake before and after the missing 2 miles of drive. To this day, I'm disappointed in myself for not verifying the time as I have an obsession with being aware of it. Prior to that incident, I loved looking at the moon, but since find myself looking at it with suspicion. I can't forget that I've experienced lost time, but I'm too afraid to undergo hypnosis to find out what really happened.

A decade later, I watched a TV show in which someone experienced something similar. Two decades after that, I worked with someone who was a UFO enthusiast and coworkers made fun of him. I told him this story, and the boss overheard and admitted that he had experienced something similar, but in Alaska. It also feels amazing to know I'm not alone.

FIRST GRADE TULPAS

John Francis Enright

Retired Software Architect

Wichita Falls, Texas, 1962

I grew up on the family farm, but during my first grade year, we moved to Wichita Falls, where my dad earned his teaching degree. This was a trying time, because I was adjusting both to school and my first exposure to urban living. I was really out of my depth, but I made my first friend early in the school year. Living in rural west Texas is a pretty lonely way to grow up, and I was struggling to learn how to interact with kids my age that weren't close family.

My new friend lived only a couple of doors down and across the street, so we walked home together every day. One afternoon, he began telling me about the monster that lived in his yard. At the time, I was amazed by all the new and strange things I encountered on a continuous basis, but this story took hold of my imagination completely. For days, I pestered him every afternoon for more details and a chance to see the beast.

He finally relented and we headed to his house to go monster hunting. The yard had been fenced in stages, and the detached garage had an isolated plot of ground along one side. There was a narrow strip with no gate or other entry point. This was the domain of the monster. We quietly crept to the corner and peeked around; the tension was explosive. What I saw was bipedal and generally reptilian. It was standing upright with basic human proportions, though it was only as large as a petite woman. Its hide was more or less dark, dull green, but mottled with brown and dark grey in a tight, busy pattern. The creature turned as we watched, as if we'd been heard. It stepped toward us, and we both screamed and ran for our lives, he to his house and me to mine. My mom finally calmed me down, and a short while later, we headed back to the farm for the weekend.

I grew up with monsters; there are plenty of animals in the woods capable of killing a six-year-old. I personally was lucky despite having encountered several. I knew monsters and the one in my neighbor's yard was unidentifiable; I'd seen it clearly, in good light, up close. I decided I needed more information, so I decided to quiz my buddy about what exactly he'd seen.

I never saw him again. My friend's family moved over the weekend I had been visiting the farm. Eventually I worked up the nerve to investigate on my own. No monster, no sign of it having ever been there. But I had seen something, clearly and unambiguously.

Decades had passed and I had decided that I must have tricked my young self. I had never forgotten the experience, and I'd given up trying to understand it, or even classify what I had seen. However one night in 2008, it was late and I was preparing for bed. The house was completely dark except for my bedroom light. When I opened the bathroom door, I was confronted by the same monster I'd seen in my youth. The reptilian man was standing in my living room, across the hall, not six feet away.

I have studied a great deal hoping to better understand these experiences. I have chosen to ignore the thing hoping that it might go away. So far it seems that it has.

SLAMMING SMOKES

Roland Ruth

Programmer

Mt. Prospect, Illinois, 2002

My girlfriend is from the Philippines, and the culture celebrates death anniversaries. It was her mom's death anniversary; her sister was over and they were going to go to church to pray for their mom. They were on the main floor of the house looking for a pack of cigarettes and lighter. I was told it was the sister's, but found out later it was my girlfriend's, as she was hiding the fact she was still smoking. They looked everywhere for the cigarettes and could not find them. They left for church and I headed down to the basement to watch some television. About 15 minutes later, I heard a loud sound from upstairs. I walked up, and right next to the basement door was the pack of cigarettes and the lighter! It wasn't near anything it could have fallen off of. I also don't understand how a pack of cigarettes and a lighter made such a loud noise...unless something slammed them down onto the floor.

SCAREDY-CAT

Cindy Acosta

Sacramento, California, 1999

My friend Mike and I were heading out to clean up a house that an old lady had died in. It was around 7:00 p.m. when we left for Austin Street. A friend's mom lived just across the field from it, so we parked there and walked over. It was a really big job, so I started at one end of the home and Mike at the other.

When we initially walked in, the smell was pretty bad; it smelled of death. As we threw things in garbage bags, we came across jars packed full of money. We opened one of the jars and touched the bills, they instantly turned to dust! Immediately a picture fell off the wall, slamming into the floor. I was starting to get scared and it was dark outside now, but Mike insisted that it was nothing and that we needed to continue doing our job. I told him that I felt like someone or something was in there with us, and that I was getting really uncomfortable. Finally he admitted that he was scared too, and we headed into the kitchen.

On the kitchen table stood a cat that had its back arched, with its hair on end, huge eyes open, and teeth bared. It was standing there but it was dead. I don't know what had happened to make a cat die like that, but it looked like it had been scared to death. I ran for my life, across the field to my friend's mom's house and never returned.

DAVID

Sonja Barclift

Retired

San Diego, California, 1975

I rented a room in a home with four San Diego State students. Shortly after moving in, strange things started happening. I would find objects like pens or coat hangers under the bottom sheet of my bed. When I removed them, they would re-appear in the same place a short time later. I began to think that I might have a ghost in my room, so I meditated and saw in my mind's eye a young man named David. He had long, dark hair and was trying to present me with a flower. In the following weeks, the presence became overbearing. I finally broke down and mentioned it to one of my roommates. He asked if my ghost had a name and I told him David. The blood drained from his face, and he got up, left the room, and returned with a photo of a young man with long dark hair. I advised him that yes, this looked like my ghost. He told me that the photo was of his brother David who had died in my room of a drug overdose. No one wanted to tell me about it for fear that I would not want to rent the room. I obtained a book from the library on hauntings and followed the instructions for releasing spirits into the light. I performed the ritual and was never bothered by David again.

DEATH WAS LAUGHING!

Tracy Wendling

Accounts Payable

Seattle, Washington, 1993

A friend brought a vintage William Fuld Ouija board to a party. We began to use the board and it was working, but everyone thought we were pushing the planchette. The spirit had identified itself as "Death." To prove we weren't pushing it, I asked it to spell out a bystander's mother's maiden name. My friend and I closed our eyes as the planchette moved around the board spelling something. It stopped moving; I opened my eyes and was shocked to see everyone's eyes and mouths wide open. My friend across the board was holding her hands up by her shoulders; I had spelled the name correctly by myself! I couldn't help but think of *The Exorcist*! Now that we had everyone's attention, we proceeded to ask Death what it wanted. He asked to meet us at an intersection that was about six blocks from our location. I had to convince most of the six people to go, as they didn't want to meet Death. It was around midnight, and we timidly made our way to the crossroads, expecting a metro bus to jump the curb and hit us, or the ground to open up and swallow us. We ended up purchasing snacks at the store at the intersection and returned home. When we returned, we got Death back on the

Ouija board and asked what had happened? He spelled "H-A-H-A-H-A." Death was laughing! We were done with the Ouija for the night!

Recently I was researching reverse speech and "death" backward is "Satan." I actually drive through that intersection every day on my way to work. It scares me even more now thanks to this revelation!

ONLY A PTERODACTYL FITS THE BILL

Lawrence Jaglarski

Floor Cleaning Services

Woodridge, Illinois, 1995

I walked out onto the balcony of my apartment to smoke. It was approximately 12:30 a.m., and I heard a loud, low whistling sound, as if a big wind was picking up. It was then that I saw what I can only describe as a pterodactyl! It was huge and it flew right past my balcony, not five or six feet from me. It was so close that I could see its big black eye focus on me. Its eye didn't move; it just sort of focused on me. The "bird" was gray and had no feathers, just small scales. Its head and neck were not stretched out looking down, like you see in science books and museums. Instead it held its head like a pelican, with its neck bent in such a way that the base of its skull rested on its back bone. It didn't flap its big wings; it simply glided. Moments later, it was gone.

I was shocked. I stood there trying to figure out what I had just seen. I went inside and told my wife what I saw, but she didn't care about my experience. I didn't have a computer back then, but have since gone online and looked for some birds that might have appeared similarly to what I saw; only a pterodactyl fits the bill!

THE OLD LADY CAME BACK

Kerry Ainsworth

Personal Assistant/Administration

Noraville, New South Wales, Australia, 2009

This happened a few weeks after I had moved into the house where I still live. It was Tuesday night, and I had gone to bed at my usual time. At about 3:00 a.m., I woke up suddenly, feeling freezing cold right through to my bones. I was horrified to realize that I was not alone in my bed; there was a really old, skinny, white haired lady lying next to me! I can't begin to tell you how freaked out I was. I jumped up and ran out of the room, too scared to go back for the rest of the night. The next morning when I dared to venture back into the room, everything seemed normal and the old lady was gone.

A couple of days later, a neighbor mentioned that the old woman, who owned my house before me, had passed away in the nursing home on the previous Tuesday night. On hearing this, I went cold all over and felt creeped out again as I realized that it was her old room that I was sleeping in.

I have never had another such experience and I can only assume that old lady came back to visit her home at the time of her passing. My blood still runs cold whenever I remember this experience.

THE CHORD OF ANNIHILATION

Betty Jean Jordan

Prepper

Keuka Lake, New York, 1964

In the corner, against the wall, sat our old up-right piano. My family did everything they could to dampen the loudness of the piano, including installing special ceiling tiles.

One evening as my parents played cards with another couple above the piano room, I struck the keys in a chord. The sound that resonated not only shattered the lenses of my special shatter-proof physical education glasses, but completely annihilated them; they disappeared! I took off the glasses and looked at the empty space in amazement! I went upstairs and told everyone that they wouldn't believe what just happened...and they didn't!

Needless to say, my mother was angry to have to replace the lenses. Even into adulthood she found my story unbelievable. I am grateful the shards of glass didn't get into my eyes and where the lenses disappeared to still remains a mystery.

A GREEN T-SHIRT

Susan Coronel

Retired

Ensanada, Mexico, 2003

My dad had passed away in 1998, and my son Roberto was too young to be able to remember him. Roberto was playing outside, and came in and said, "I seen Pa." My dad was commonly called Pa. I asked, "What was he wearing?" because my dad only wore jeans and white t-shirts. Roberto said he was wearing jeans and a green t-shirt. I said to myself, "Well that wasn't Dad; he only wears white t-shirts." I was on the phone telling my sister about it, and I said I knew it wasn't Dad because he didn't have a white t-shirt on. My sister said, "Susan, Dad was going to the doctor the morning he died. He wanted to dress up a little and so put on a green t-shirt, and then had a heart attack."

NIGHT FISHING

Matt Mattox

Retired

Lake Mead, Nevada, 2002

My buddy and I went to Nevada from Wichita, to fish at Lake Mead and play golf. We drove his van and used his 18-foot boat. We didn't catch any fish while fishing during the day. We fished for several days, but had no luck anywhere, at any depth. We started golfing in the later part of the day, then decided to come back to Wichita.

That night, as we were getting the boat ready to load onto the trailer, we saw many big fish in the water at the marina. I suggested that we try fishing at night, so around 8:00 p.m., we went out. When we started fishing, it was pretty dark. We trolled back and forth for an hour or so, and could see millions of stars. Quickly and un-expectedly, a bright light came out of the lake! I pointed it out to my buddy, and he was able to see it just be-fore it vanished from sight. Years later, I saw a program about USOs (Unidentified Submerged Objects) on tele-vision and got validation of my experience; I wasn't see-ing things or crazy! As soon as this "light" had emerged from the water, it was gone in two or three seconds!

MORNING COFFEE

René Carrero

Retired

Tampa, Florida, 2006

I was preparing my fiancée's coffee and left the spoon in the cup. As Carol emerged from her sleepy state and walked toward me out of the bedroom, we heard a tinkling, metallic sound. It was the same sound that was created by dropping a spoon into a cup from a few inches above. We glanced at each other with question marks flashing over our heads. I asked, "Did you hear that?"

"Yeah." she replied.

I went to investigate. I yelled out to Carol to come and see this unusual occurrence; the spoon I had left in the cup, laying in the normal position flat side resting on the edge of the cup had, somehow, ended up balanced on the thin edge. We stared at each other in awe. She exclaimed, "Ghosts?!"

I, and my goose bumps, said, "Nahhh!" as I coordinated the appropriate hand gesture, indicating disbelief. We sat quietly across from each other trying to replicate what had just happened while having our morning brew, all the while wondering whether ghosts or poltergeist really exist.

We still have no idea how this happened.

JOANNE

Edna Walsh

Retired

Wake Forest, North Carolina, 1990

My daughter, Karen, her three young children, and I were riding along in the car on the way to do some shopping. As was the usual practice, we played word games or indulged the kids in answering the myriad questions which they came up with, in order to entertain them and to keep the peace.

On this particular outing, we were trying to explain that people just didn't pop into being; first they had to be a little baby and then grow to be an adult over a period of time. My granddaughter, Katie, went into a trance-like state and started speaking in a very clear voice (not her usual mode of speaking). She said, "I used to be a little baby once. My name was Joanne. Then I crossed over." She immediately reverted back to her usual behavior. Chills went down my spine as I had had a sister named Joanne who died in infancy. Her name was never brought up, so there was no reason for Katie to have picked up that name. No one in their circle had that name. In fact, my other adult children knew vaguely that I had a sister who died in infancy but they didn't know her name.

Another strange incident happened a short time later in my home. My youngest grandchild, Brooke, was a little more than 1 year old. She was sitting in her highchair observing the goings-on as the family was all gathered together. I was standing several feet from her. The subject of Katie bringing up the name Joanne came up and I turned to the baby Brooke and said jokingly, "What is going on in that little head of yours? Where did you come from?" She responded with an enigmatic smile and then a jagged streak of light flew from her solar plexus into mine. I was shocked. I am now definitely a believer in reincarnation!

I DECIDED I WOULD JUMP

Linda Gale

Retired Respiratory Therapist

Denver, Colorado, June 1986

While riding in the car with my husband in June 1986, I had a daydream about what I would do if I was crossing the street and was about to be hit by a car. I decided that I would jump to protect my knees.

Fast forward to December 16, 1988 at around 4:15 p.m. I was struck by a car while walking home from the post office. I was momentarily knocked out, my body landed 25 feet from the scene, and when I became conscious, the driver of the car (who had stopped along with many others) said: "You jumped so high!" The accident happened at the exact same location where I had the daydream two years prior. I was about two blocks from my home on the street on which I lived. The car was a gray Mercedes, and my knee caps would have been destroyed if I had not jumped.

MY HAUNTED FARM

Cheryl McAtee

Retired

Vancouver, Washington, 1992

My move to my dream farm in April 1992 quickly turned into a greater money pit than I had estimated. It was just me, two large protective dogs, and three cats in the house.

The work on my 1880s farm house started in June, as did the unexplainable happenings. I would hear steps up the stairs at night. The doors would lock when I went outside on rainy nights. Things would go missing and then reappear. My television would turn off while I slept, and I'd hear noises in my lower attic that sounded like racoons wrestling, though nothing would be there. The second time I was locked out, I asked whatever it was to please not do that to me again. It stopped.

That October, during a lovely fall afternoon, I was on the back porch painting shutters propped below the kitchen windows. As I happened to glance at the window, I noticed a handsome man standing about 20 feet behind me with a bemused expression. At first I wondered how he could have opened the gate to the property without my hearing him and alerting the dogs. He was dressed in a brown duster with a beaver skin hat and long riding pants and boots. He had longish brown hair. I turned to look at him, but he wasn't there! I turned back to the window, but his reflection had disappeared as well.

Things continued to happen, and though my dogs and cats would pay attention to the noises, they did not react to them. I hadn't thought much about ghosts until I moved here. I think it was a protective ghost that was watching over the renovations and approved.

About 12 years ago, I met the author of a book on ghost stories in the county. I told him some of my stories, and he asked if he could visit. When he did, he said he sensed a presence, but it did not have bad intentions.

I'm still here, but not much has happened recently.

THE THING UNDER THE TRUCK

Justin Tucker

Digital Photo Retoucher/Professional Skydiver

Cornwall, New York, 1998

Late one summer night, around 2 a.m., my best friend Rob and I were walking down the sidewalk on a street near my home in the rural neighborhood where I grew up. We never walked anywhere—we skateboarded—but they had recently re-paved this particular street in the tar-and-gravel fashion which made our preferred method of travel all but impossible. The sidewalk was no better of an option as it was cracked, crumbling, overgrown, and in a state of upheaval due to the roots of the large oak trees that lined the street. Even before the recent repavement, this street was poorly maintained, so we always had to walk it, and being that only one side of the street had a sidewalk, we always walked the same boring and painfully slow side.

On the opposite side of the street there was a small house with a large pick-up truck in the driveway. Out of the corner of my eye, I saw something run under the truck that caused Rob and me to freeze. Whatever it was, it set off the motion detector that caused the outdoor light above the garage to turn on. It wasn't the movement that startled us to a dead stop; rather, it was the way the creature moved. It was bipedal and appeared to be a hairless, yellowish-flesh color. Neither of us said a word as we stood frozen looking at the area of darkness under the truck where this thing had disappeared.

The pick-up truck had a lift kit installed in it and massive tires, much larger and wider than normal ones. The body of the truck sat a good deal higher than a typical vehicle would. The driveway was well lit by the flood light which was mounted above the garage of the house. After a few terrifying seconds, two hands appeared on the inside edge of the truck's rear tire. It placed its fingers down in a creepy, one-at-a-time fashion, pinkies first followed by ring, middle, then index. Finally, the creature's head peeked out to see if we were still there. The bald, earless, round head slowly appeared until its large, yellowish eyes made contact with ours. It quickly ducked back into the shadow of the truck.

Rob and I shrieked like little girls and ran the remaining 50 feet to the intersection at the end of the road where we could hop on our skateboards and get the hell out of there. We skated as fast as we could for a quarter mile or so, and then stopped to catch our breath and then asked each other over and over, "What the hell was that thing?!" and "Dude, did you see that thing? What the hell was it?!" We confirmed with each other that we did indeed see the same thing and that neither of us had a clue what it was. It resembled the little alien in the movie *Mac & Me*, except it wasn't as cute, clumsy, and dumpy looking. It was more slender and creepy. The next day, we agreed that we weren't going to tell anyone what had happened because we didn't think anyone would believe us. If someone had told us the same story, we probably wouldn't have believed them either.

This event set me on a path of curiosity that continues and intensifies with every passing day.

HAPPY BIRTHDAY

Shelley Wright

Numismatist

Asheville, North Carolina

A couple of years ago, I called my best friend Beth and sang "Happy Birthday" to her, as I did every year. We chatted a few minutes longer, making dinner plans for later that evening, but I got the feeling that something was bothering her. She just didn't sound right.

We met and ate dinner and she opened her presents. We were about to get up from our table when she blurted out, "I have a confession to make. When you sang Happy Birthday to me this morning, you sounded just like my mother." Her beloved mother had been dead for months.

"I have a confession to make too," I said. "I talked to your mother last night, and I asked her to do or say something that would let you know she was around and loved you."

LATE NIGHT ASSISTANT

Connie Watson

Retired

San Francisco, California, 1982

In 1982, I was working the night shift in a word processing center for Standard Oil Company on Market Street in San Francisco. We had twin high-rises next door to each other. Our office was on the third floor of 575 Market Street, and we would often go and help out in the engineering department's word processing center next door on the ninth floor of 555 Market Street. They had no night shift, so whoever went to help out would be working alone on the ninth floor.

One evening, I had gone over and left the door open to the hallway. I had turned on a radio to try to ease the creepy feeling of the place and was busily working on engineering specs. Suddenly, amid the noise of the radio and the loud noise of the printer, I felt someone walk into the room and stand next to me, as if curious about what I was doing. Every hair on my arms and the back of my neck stood up, and I was paralyzed with fear. For some reason, I didn't want whoever this ghost was to think that I was aware of them so I said aloud, "Oh no, I forgot one of the tapes." I reached down, got my purse, and refused to look up above the cubicle wall at the darkened windows because I knew if I did, I might see who was standing next to me reflected in the window.

I left everything turned on and walked to the elevators, feeling the ghost walking along with me. Waiting for that elevator was the longest few minutes of my life. I thought I was going to pass out from fright. When the elevator doors opened I stepped inside and just before I got all the way in, I felt someone lift up the back of my long hair and let it fall. The ghost did not get into the elevator with me.

I went back to my office, and the three men I worked with said I was so pale that I looked like I had seen a ghost. When I told them what had happened, all three immediately went next door to check it out. They found nothing. They turned off the lights and closed up the office for me. I never worked over there alone again. We did find out that a man had died in his office in that building a few years earlier and was not discovered until the cleaning crew came in at night.

This happened more than 30 years ago, and I still remember it like it was yesterday.

AS I GAZED AT HER

Beverly Caron

Realtor, retired

2010

How does one begin to tell a creepy story when they don't know when it happened?

It comes back to me only when I sleep. It seems to be a recurring memory of an incident that happened while my husband and I were attending a social function at our local Elks Club. The gathering was large, and I was conversing with a woman I intuitively felt I knew very well when something very startling happened; it was a momentary flash. I had the distinct impression that the person with whom I was speaking wanted me to see what I did, but didn't want me to remember it, when it happened, or even who she was.

As I gazed at her, as one does when engaged in conversation, the pupils of her eyes vertically compressed from the sides and changed to resemble those of a snake or reptilian. It seemed as though she dropped a shield which cloaked her real appearance and allowed me to see her real eyes!

There is nothing more to this story except that I see the incident often in my sleep, but it doesn't seem like a normal dream; it is always exactly the same. When I wake, I can still see a fading image of those eyes and remember that it really did happen, but no other details at all. It does not frighten me, but I'm torn between wanting to know when it happened and to whom I was speaking, and wondering what I would do even if I knew who my female reptilian friend is.

KNIVES

Melodie Stewart

Retired

Sharon, Pennsylvania, 1976

I was in my early 20s and had recently moved into a new home. I was home alone one night and, for some odd reason, had an overwhelming feeling that knives were being aimed at me. The feeling was so intense that the hair on my arms was actually standing up! I was afraid to shut my eyes because I knew the knives were floating all around and pointed directly at me ready to strike. My uncle had died not long before this occurred, and I kept feeling like he was with me; I hoped he was there to protect me. I finally fell asleep on the couch. When I woke up the next morning, all seemed fine until I got out of the shower and saw myself in the mirror. I had two razor sharp red marks slashed across my throat!

MY SISTER'S ROOM

Anne Marie Caron

Administration

Little Canada, Minnesota, 1975

One evening, when I was around 16 years old, my best friend Julie and I were having a sleepover at my house. When we kept hearing odd sounds like someone was moving about upstairs, we finally broke down and complained to my cousin Doug and our friend Bob that we were scared that someone might have broken into the house. So being big, brave boys, they took us upstairs to search for the intruder. There were five rooms, so we each took one and searched it completely. I walked out of my sister's room after satisfying myself that no one was in there. I came out into the hallway to see Bob and Julie standing in front of the rooms they had searched. I took two steps toward them when suddenly the door behind me slammed shut and someone from inside my sister's room began violently pounding on the door with all their might! We all jumped, but immediately assumed it was Doug. At that very instant, Doug walked out of my brother's room behind Julie and Bob, asking what was going on. We all looked at him, screamed and then ran over each other trying to get down the stairs. It was very funny afterward, but still very creepy. As I stated earlier, I checked every inch of my sister's room personally and found nothing. Of course finding nothing gave me no comfort whatsoever, because my bedroom was right next to my sister's!

REALLY AN ANGEL?

Gloria M. Gieseke

San Antonio, Texas, 1993

(From chapter 31 of *Where Is the Music? The Multiple Near-Death Experiences of a World Traveler* by Gloria M. Gieseke, 1999)

In 1993, at age 79, my mother's health was not bad, except for signs of a slight loss of memory. With her two granddaughters halfway through college and one of them married, she decided to sell her house and do some traveling overseas. She mostly wanted to visit my sister in Italy and me in the United States.

In the summer of 1994, she left Colombia with one of her granddaughters for a short visit to Russia and then on to Rome. At her age, we didn't want her to travel alone, so by the end of the summer, I went to Colombia to pick her up after her return from Europe and bring her with me to the United States. It was my turn to care for my mother, and I welcomed the privilege of doing it. I must confess that the idea was hers, and I was grateful she thought of it, because we tend to think or hope that our parents will live forever, and they don't.

Long talks, short walks, a little gardening, a loving Chihuahua to take a nap with, a hug and a kiss, and a game of cards were most of the simple pleasures she enjoyed. Her favorite thing to do was go to the River Walk in downtown San Antonio and take a ride on a barge. About once a month, we would take the bus and go somewhere together. We would visit churches, restaurants, malls, or even attend parades. Like me, she enjoyed shopping and the outdoors.

A strange thing happened to us one day when we were downtown. After a fair amount of walking around and shopping, my mother and I went to a restaurant to have lunch. There I noticed my coin purse was missing. It had held my student bus card and my mother's senior citizen's ID, plus about six dollars in change and small bills. I remembered having used the little purse downtown that afternoon for some change. It wasn't a big problem because I had enough money with me to pay for lunch and buses. It was just going to be an inconvenience to do paperwork and take the time to go get new ID cards. After lunch, we took the 40-minute bus ride home.

About 10 minutes into the ride, a tall woman I had never seen before got on the bus, looked at us and said, "You lost some IDs today, didn't you? I have them, and I want to return them to you. All the money is there too." In her hand she held my little orange and black cloth purse. I asked her how she knew it was ours. She answered, "By your mother's photo," and handed me the purse. Delighted to have our IDs back, I thanked her twice and said to her, "You are an angel." She moved on to take a seat two rows back on the opposite side of us. Two stops down the road she got off the bus.

That shook me up a little more; why would that woman get on the same bus hours later, far from the place where I had lost my purse? She got on the bus at the same stop my mother and I had got on the bus, seemingly just to return our IDs, then got off the bus immediately thereafter. It made no sense to me. My mother's picture on her ID wasn't a clear one and the woman had not held the picture in front of us to compare features, nor had I seen her take the time to study my mother's face (my student bus card did not have a photo on it). Was the woman really an angel? I smiled and thanked God again.

STRANGE GEOMETRY

James Alan Sanders

Security Guard

The Big Easy Tavern, Pensacola, Florida, 2011

A year or so ago, I was consuming a Guinness beer at a local favorite pub called The Big Easy. I glanced to my right and saw two big trapezoids jut from the back area from the restroom area near the pool table. They were on top of each other. The top one was bright white and approximately 2 inches, by 24 inches, by 8 feet, about 5 feet off the floor. The other one was blacker than black, the same dimensions and shape, one foot from the floor. The black one was in front of the white one (as if you walked that way you would have hit it first). Then they darted back into the direction they came from. I thought, "This is really good Guinness!"

I turned back to the bar and saw the owner's wife, Kelly, moving forward with such a look on her face, it suggested she had seen something also. I said "Did you see that?" She said, "Yes." Her husband, Chip (a retired Navy Corpsman), and I investigated. We found nothing out of the ordinary. I asked Kelly what she saw and proceeded to describe the shapes. Kelly agreed with my description. Chip and Kelly never drank while working, and Chip, being a Navy Corpsman, is not to be doubted.

I have seen these trapezoids subsequently, but to a lesser degree.

THE SOUL STEALER

Jennifer Kough

Secretary

Howell, Michigan, 2007

It was the summer of 2007, and I was sleeping over at my boyfriend Billy's house. When we would go to bed, he'd always sleep by the wall and I'd sleep on the outside.

I awoke to the door creaking as it opened. I laid there looking at a very tall, dark figure standing in the doorway. Billy started tapping me with his finger. The dark figure entered the room and gazed at us for a moment. Suddenly it crouched down on all fours and started running around the bed, back and forth, growling and snarling. It had shifted into something like a dog. This thing looked blacker than the darkest shadows in the bedroom. I couldn't believe what I was seeing, and my boyfriend was tapping me faster now. I was paralyzed with fear so all I could do was watch the creature on the floor. It stopped at the foot of the bed, jumped up, and clamped its jaws on Billy's foot and yanked him halfway off of the bed! Billy sat up as the creature backed into the darkest corner of the room and disappeared. Billy and I spoke about what had happened, and he told me he couldn't move or talk when the creature touched him. He said he was trying to call out to me, but no sound would come out. We tried to sleep. The next day we saw that there were bruises around Billy's ankle.

This incident baffles us to this day. Billy thinks the creature was trying to steal his soul and jump into his body. Billy's mom thinks it was a demon, the same demon that had taken over her father when she was young. Her father was a very evil man that had molested children and beat his family. When she was a little girl, her father was locked in the house as it burned to the ground. I don't know what to make of this as I've had shadow figure encounters, but nothing violent like this. I do know this thing was after something.

A STRANGE, OMINOUS FEELING

Micarla Tolbert

Disabled/Painter

Martins Ferry, Ohio, 1993 to 2000

As is common these days, my parents divorced when I was young. My siblings and I lived primarily with our mother and visited Dad's house every other weekend. Shortly after the divorce, I moved from the old family house on the hill to one in town with my mom, sister, and brother. The new house was previously a duplex, but had been converted into a four bedroom, one family home. It was lovely.

All was normal for the longest time, until unbeknownst to each other, my siblings and I each began having experiences in the house. We all frequently got creepy feelings, especially at night, but we also each had our own, unique experiences.

My brother's bedroom was close to one of the two bathrooms and didn't have air conditioning or the heating duct work completed. He frequently slept with his door open at night. He regularly heard someone walking up the staircase, go into the bathroom, and turn the shower on. This happened like clockwork, between 2:00 and 3:00 a.m. My sister, whose room was directly across the hall, never heard a thing. Finally one night, my brother gathered the courage to investigate. He got out of bed, went to the bathroom, flipped on the light and pulled open the shower curtain. No one was there and the shower was dry.

My sister had her own instances of strange activity. She and I actually had similar experiences but didn't know it. There would be times we would be in our rooms and decide to go downstairs for a late-night snack or glass of water. We would stop on the landing, smack-dab in the middle of the staircase, and would experience the exact same phenomenon as our brother. Both my sister and I would turn around and head back to our rooms. Again, this would happen regularly to each of us, but we didn't know the others were having experiences. When we later found out, we would stop and go back to our bedrooms for the very same reasons. We would get a strange, ominous feeling, like there was something downstairs; I would get cold chills. Everybody would be upstairs and asleep at these times, so no one was downstairs.

It wasn't until years later that we found out that an elderly woman had lived in one half of the duplex and apparently committed suicide in the basement. Is this the person my brother would hear every night, coming up the stairs to take a shower? Is she the reason my sister and I would refuse to go downstairs some nights, even for a drink of water? We may never know.

THE CHILDREN AND THE REPTILIANS

Doug

Truck Driver

Fairborn, Ohio, and Colorado Springs, Colorado,
1965–1970

I was haunted by uninvited visitors from the time I was 3 until I was 8, while my family lived at Wright Patterson Air Force Base and then at the U.S. Air Force Academy. I was abducted at least three times when I was 5, and my sister and some neighborhood kids had similar experiences. The visitors my sister and I encountered in Ohio were reptilian; I was about 4 and she was about 3 years old. We told our parents there was a snake because we knew what snakes were, as we had a long toy snake made out of round sheets of colored plastic. We called the toy "Niki," because one day I asked it its name and it told me. Looking back, now I wonder if it was an Anunnaki. The reptilians would examine us and pat us on our faces. They were tall, green, and scaly with arms and legs, a tail and yellow slanted eyes. More peculiar was that they would appear wearing a hat similar to those mobsters would wear in the 1950s.

One abduction that stands out in my memory happened at the U.S. Air Force Academy. I was 5. I remember seeing a flash of light, and then I was in a stainless steel hospital-like environment screaming for my mom. Yelling seemed to hurt their ears, and I saw tall and short grey aliens here as well as human doctors in white doctor's uniforms. I could see but could not move; I was paralyzed. They put me to sleep with some object because they wanted me to stop screaming. Then it was the usual testing. I remember walking into a waiting room and seeing other terrified humans, then the next thing I recalled was falling. They put it in my head I was an astronaut, and I actually felt the wind, as I fell, thinking I was going to hit the ground. I landed in my bed on feathers softly, the feathers blowing up in the air all around me. I awoke and sat upright. I never slept on my back so I knew it wasn't a dream.

The next morning, I asked my mom why she didn't help me when she had to have heard me screaming bloody murder the previous night. Mom and Dad had not heard a thing. I asked why they didn't save me. They responded by telling me I had just had a nightmare. As I walked down the hall to breakfast, I had a strange sensation, as if I was very groggy from having been drugged. I asked some of the neighborhood kids if they ever had dreams or nightmares, and some said yes. One girl even described the exact same things happening to her that had happened to me. Some nights we would knock on the telephone pole and ask "Niki" to not attack us that night. Sometimes we would taunt him, and those nights we would be attacked.

BANGING FROM ABOVE

Jesse Garza

Artist

Savannah, Georgia, 2005

Back when I was in college, I worked at the local radio station for the Savannah College of Art and Design. One night after I completed my shift around 2:00 a.m., I called the student bus to take me back to campus. The student radio station was located at Key's Hall, which had formally been the Savannah TV station. While I was waiting for the bus to take me home, I heard a loud thump emanate from the hallway above me. I ignored it, figuring it was just my imagination. As I continued to wait, the thumping continued to get louder and closer to where I was in the lobby.

The thumping was occurring in sets of two, each time getting closer to me and getting louder. I began to worry. The thumping sound echoed, immediately above me. At that point, I gathered my belongings and exited the building. The student bus came and picked me up, and I reported what I had heard. Campus security came, investigated the building ,and confirmed that I had been there alone. The bus driver on the way home told me that several facility members refused to work in that building, and many custodians and service folks had reported the same incident. I never again encountered anything similar to what I did that night in the building.

SMALL-TOWN SURPRISE

Rich

Construction

Chatuagua County, New York, 2002

On a beautiful summer's day in August, my agenda was to investigate a curious place. I was living in New York state at the time, and a friend had told me of a place not far away that I should never visit. Of course, this only made me want go.

So with perfect weather and not a cloud in the sky, I hopped in the car and drove. I found the place easily; it was called Lily Dale. Even though this town was renowned for having the highest concentration of psychics and mediums in the world, it was a small place, with a seemingly private community. I drove around looking at everything, including the little, old homes and the small streets.

I was about ready to leave when three women started crossing the street in front of me. They were about 100 feet away, but as I looked at them, I saw something much more; I saw three entities occupying the space immediately around them. I blinked my eyes a number of times and couldn't believe what I was seeing. As the women crossed the street, they looked at me while the entities surrounding them were staring with red, glowing eyes. It was noon on a very bright and sunny day, and what I saw I was actually witnessing, not just imagining. Just as they reached the curb on other side, I heard a voice speaking in my mind and it said, "Now, do you believe?"

I answered, "Yes, without a doubt."

I left as soon as they did.

STRANGE SAVIOR

Max Cooper

Information Technology/Information Systems

Kuwait

I was about 5 or 6 years old when I tried to run across an expressway, and I guess I was not running fast enough. I got run over by a truck but some beings saved me. I heard them contemplating whether or not I was worth saving. Finally one of them said to the others that yes, I should be saved. I then became fully conscious and found my body perfectly aligned under the truck so that nothing had actually happened to me; I was completely uninjured.

Both my brother and I used to hear and see these beings.

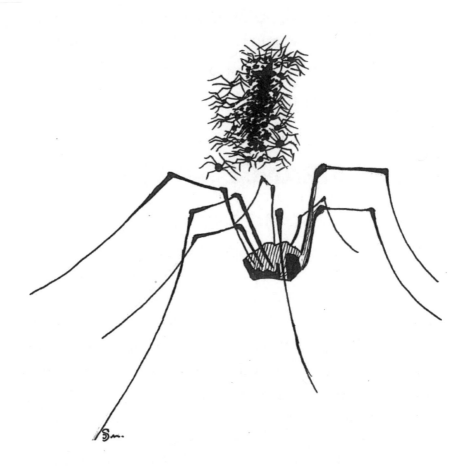

DADDY LONGLEGS

Thomas L. Hancock

Bryce Creek, Oregon, 2008

In September 2008, my grandmother, who I was very close to, died at 99 years old. Being so close to her, I knew that her very favorite animal in the whole world, oddly enough, was the daddy longleg spider. She loved to watch them and it was not uncommon to see her letting them dance, gangly, across her fingers.

Just weeks after Grandma's passing, I went on a hunting trip with a friend of mine. We found a nice secluded area and set up camp. We started our fire just before dark, and we started talking about my grandma. For whatever reason, I had always favored saying goodbye to loved ones that had passed by getting back to nature as opposed to attending a funeral, so this seemed like the perfect time to reminisce about her and say my goodbyes.

About an hour into our conversation, we both noticed that it looked like the ground was moving. We turned on our head lamps to see the entire campsite and the bottom of our pants legs entirely covered with daddy longlegs! I would say that an area of about 10 feet by 10 feet was completely covered by them. I was so overwhelmed with strong feelings and thoughts of Grandma that it almost seemed she was there with me. We let the little creatures be and just kept talking as they crawled everywhere.

After about 30 minutes of this, we decided to go to our separate tents and get some sleep. The daddy long-legs were still everywhere, covering the ground. After about 10 minutes, my friend had to get up, as nature called. He turned on his head lamp, stepped out of his tent and found mine completely covered with the daddy longlegs. There were none on his tent or around the area we were sitting before. As his light shined on my tent, all I could see were hundreds of spindly shadows. The next morning when we got up, we saw no sign of the daddy longlegs anywhere. This was the only night this happened to us during the 10 days we stayed at this site.

TEENAGE GUEST

Stuart Jennings

Toolmaker

Fuengirola, Spain, 2008

I was five days into a weeklong vacation with my partner and her two young teenage girls. When I awoke around 3:00 a.m., the apartment was nicely lit by a combination of moonlight and streetlight streaming through the patio windows in the other room. I rolled over toward my partner, and to my surprise, the shadowy figure of a young teenage girl wandered from the other room into the hallway directly outside our bedroom doorway.

I couldn't make out any details of her face, but I could clearly see that she had shoulder-length, mousy brown hair. She was wearing some sort of nightgown or long shirt, and was rubbing her hair with one hand as if she was lost or sleepwalking. I immediately assumed it was one of the kids looking for the toilet, even though they were both in a different apartment. Before I had a chance to speak or do anything, she turned round and silently wandered back into the main room.

My partner was lying awake on her back beside me, so I nudged her and asked, "Is one of the kids sleeping in here?" She replied, "No, there is no one in here except for us." Of course I then said, "Well, someone just walked through that doorway!"

I then turned on the light and spent the next 10 minutes searching the apartment from top to bottom. I was so sure that I would find someone in there that I was preparing to defend myself if necessary. Once I had completed my search without finding anyone, I returned to bed shaking like a leaf with every hair on my body standing on end. I knew that there was no way anyone had gone out through the front door, as it was locked and made a loud noise when it opened. The young person I had seen had walked off in the other direction opposite the front door. That left only the fifth-floor balcony to contend with. I was sure she had not gone that way, as to climb over the balcony would have been suicidal. Besides, she looked half asleep when I saw her, and there was no noise at all. I spent the next half hour lying in bed with my hand on the light switch, wondering what the hell I had witnessed, before eventually falling asleep.

I KNEW IT WAS MAX

Barney Cissell

Homeland Security

47th General Army Hospital, Frankfurt, Germany, 1990

Let me begin by stating that I have always been "sensitive" to spiritual matters. I could pass an automobile accident and intuitively know if someone had died; it's something I just could never explain and eventually, I simply shrugged it off, as none of my experiences were ever anything personal or sensational.

It was in 1990; I was an x-ray technician at an army hospital in Germany. Every morning, I had to take a chest x-ray on a sergeant. (I'll call him Max.) He had been a victim of exposure to a gas grenade and had been in a coma for several weeks in the intensive care unit.

One night while I was working the graveyard shift, a code blue, medical emergency was called for the intensive care unit. I knew it was Max. I rushed over with my portable x-ray machine ready to go to work. Drapes covered the windows and the door was closed to his room. It was filled with doctors and nurses. I stood outside of the room waiting and after about 15 minutes, I suddenly felt weird. A warm wave seemed to come, and I saw a white formless face which was undoubtedly the spirit of Max. As it came toward me, I could feel what he was thinking; he was in disbelief that this was happening to him! He then went through my head and exited upward. A few seconds later, a nurse came out of the room and I asked her if she was going to need me. She said no, that he had just passed. I went back to my department shaken by the event.

THUNDER IN THE SPEAKERS

Richard Eugene Delbridge

Retired

Southern Indiana, 2013

It was late June when I heard thunder coming from my computer speakers. It started a week ago when I was listening to a *Coast to Coast AM* on YouTube. I thought it came from George Noory's studio, so I replayed that portion of the conversation, but it wasn't there. Later that day, a thunderstorm came through my area. A few days later, a series of thunderstorms blew through, and it happened again three more times: the thunder was clearly coming from the speakers. In fact, I lost my Internet connection and put on a movie when the last one occurred.

PSYCHOSOMATIC

Ashu M. G. Solo

Interdisciplinary Research and Development Engineer and Mathematician

A small town in Arizona, 2005

I had been driving for a very long time, so I decided to take an overnight break and get some sleep. I had been sleeping in the driver's seat of my car with my seat leaned back in a parking lot, when I had a very vivid and violent dream. I dreamed I was in a vicious fight with someone in a garage. My attacker grabbed my arm, put vice grips on it, and painfully tightened them. I awoke suddenly and had severe pain in my arm. It stayed sore for most of the next day.

Either the pain carried over from real life to my dream, or the pain from my dream manifested into real life. Perhaps my arm was in a bad position and in pain while I was sleeping and this is what caused me to dream that my arm was put into vice grips. On the other hand, perhaps I felt physical pain as a result of being attacked in my dream. Did the body affect the mind, or did the mind affect the body?

THE PEN

Alexandra Fulsang

Information Clerk

Hornby, Ontario, Canada, 2000

I was in my kitchen cooking dinner and doing other tasks, when I began writing a note on a piece of paper. I put the pen I was using down on the counter and went back to cooking. After tending to the food, I turned back to continue with my note, but I could not find my pen. I knew I had just put it down, so I searched over and over, retracing my steps but still unable to locate my pen. I finally gave up, grabbed another pen, and forgot about the missing one.

A couple of weeks later, I set a pot of water to boil on the stove. I checked to see how it was doing, and in it was the pen that had disappeared a few weeks previously! I said out loud, "Ha, ha, very funny!"

To this day I have no idea who or what was playing with me.

THE SILHOUETTE

Joel Klinkner

College Student

Clearwater, Minnesota, 2009

Ever since my grandma had her house built, relatives have claimed to see shadows moving in the basement, but only when they are alone. People also have claimed to hear voices in the upstairs spare bedroom of two people talking.

Several years ago, I spent the night at Grandma's house and was sleeping downstairs in a spare room in the basement. There is no door to the room, only a curtain. I remember waking up and seeing the dark silhouette of a person standing in the doorway with the curtain wide open. Behind the silhouette I could see colors of purple and red, and could hear a humming, buzzing noise that sounded similar to a dentist's drill. I was fully conscious and aware of my surroundings, but I couldn't move or scream.

The dark shadow of what looked like a person moved closer to the bed until it was right next to me. When it gazed down at me, I finally was able to move so I grasped what was close—my cellphone—and threw it at it. In that very second, I realized my assault hadn't even fazed it. All I could do was retreat under my covers and try to quickly move away from the being. I emerged from under my blankets on the opposite side of the bed and realized in an instant that the dark shadow was gone. My cellphone was back where it was, as if I had never thrown it. The curtain was shut and the strange noise had stopped. It was as if I had been dreaming, but if it was a dream, I felt as if I had been fully conscious through all of it. I had trouble falling back to sleep after all of this had happened. Luckily it only occurred the one time. To this day, it still gives me chills when I think about that night.

A HAUNTED FAMILY

Sean Perry

Student

Lynnwood, Washington, 2002–2012

My family, which consisted of my brother, sister, mom, dad, and me, moved into our newly built house in a small community known as Willowick Lane. Three of my family members, including myself, are specially attuned to the spiritual world by means of intuition and, in some cases, the ability to sense the dead. With such talents also come great risks and extremes. Through nearly a decade, my mom, my sister, and I all dealt with very terrifying haunts while my father and brother sat back and watched without sharing our ability.

One day after school, I walked home from the bus stop and found that I was alone in the house. Every light was on, which was peculiar because we were all trained to turn off the lights before leaving the house unattended. My cat was hiding in a corner alone, which was very odd considering his usual social habits whenever I would come home. Because we are a very eco-friendly bunch, I turned off any lights I was not using and went to the upstairs bathroom. There was a loud bang against the wall of the bathroom that backs onto the hallway. This didn't bother me until I opened the bathroom door to find every light turned on in the house again—every light that I had turned off moments before.

For several months, I had struggled with turning off the light in my room and traveling from the kitchen through the hallway. I also found it challenging to take the ascent up the stairs to my room in the middle of the second floor. This was especially troubling considering I had several late night shows that I watched. Every night, I experienced the same chill down my spine when I'd leave the kitchen, and I swore to myself I did not see that shadow apparition in the kitchen after the lights fell dark. I also tried convincing myself that the creaking sound that would follow me up the stairs was simply either poor construction or the house settling. Once in my room, I would shut the door quickly and hope to be free of the terror. Instead, my room would turn into a prison. Several nights I woke up from a minor trance, as I attempted to battle fear and anxiety of turning off the lights, and praying myself to sleep. One night I became aware that I had been standing with my finger on the light switch for over two hours before regaining consciousness.

In 2008, I found my sister standing by the front windows of the house staring out the window, but her eyes were completely blank as though she were staring into nothingness. I tapped her on the shoulder and asked her if she was okay. She replied, "I thought someone was staring at me through the window from the porch." We spoke some more and she insisted that there was a strange feeling of being watched by something she couldn't see. She too found herself frozen around the house in various locations completely unconscious of what she was doing.

During the same year, I suffered from extremely terrifying dreams. In my dream, I would wake up in a dark room with doors that were locked in from the other side, and lights with switches that did not work. I was in a place of total hopelessness, and I could not voluntarily wake up. Two years later, I encountered an entity in this dream much more dark than any abyss I had ever seen. It was totally absent of light and form, approaching me and feeding on my fear. With what felt like my entire soul being devoured, I did the only thing I could do: I prayed to God. The pleading desperation of my prayers only mocked the shadow being, as it continued to approach as I repeated, "In the name of God, be gone." The more I said this, the more I began to believe in my words, and eventually the shadow being retreated. When I awoke from this dream, having spent what seemed to be an eternity trapped, it would turn out to be a few minutes after 3:00 a.m.

Although the being had retreated, it returned three more times to test me. Each time the darkness returned, I would become stronger in ensuring the defeat of this spirit. My sister did eventually move out of our home, but a darkness followed her from one house to another until she eventually learned how to fight it off and protect her son. My mom, however, had already defeated this demon decades before we had to fight our own battles.

I know my own children will face this threat, and I will prepare them in the way I wish I had been done for myself. I defeated the evil, but it doesn't stop because it has lost against an individual. It simply finds another to taunt.

THE HAND

Tanjrina Arena

Freelance Copywriter/Proofreader

Enon Valley, Pennsylvania, 1995

When I was 8 years old, back in 1995, I was living with my grandparents in their rural home in Enon Valley, Pennsylvania. They had a spare room that was used as my playroom. All of my toys were in there, including my Barbie dolls and Barbie Dream House.

One day, I was in my playroom playing by myself while my grandma was sitting in the living room and my grandpa was at work. Suddenly, I saw a disembodied hand appear out of thin air over the top of my Barbie Dream House. The hand was much larger than my then child-sized hand; it was closer to the size of an adult's hand. If the hand had a visible arm or body attached to it, it was hidden behind the dollhouse, out of my view. I was frozen with terror as I watched the fingers of the disembodied hand rapidly dance as it quickly moved back and forth, from one side of the dollhouse's roof to the other. Finally, I stood up screaming and ran out of the room to my grandma.

I never saw the disembodied hand again after that, but I will never forget it. I often wonder if it was a ghost haunting my dollhouse that day, or perhaps some kind of trickster entity visited me. I'll never know.

SCARED YOU, DIDN'T I?

Stone Wallace

Writer/Novelist

Rural Community, Northern Manitoba, Canada, early 1970s

Some years back, I hosted a local television program called *Tales of the Supernatural*, and during a show on ghosts and hauntings, I was told a particularly eerie, unexplainable story that to this day sends a chill through me.

Sheila was a young woman who took a job teaching elementary classes at a rural one-room schoolhouse in northern Manitoba. She boarded with an elderly lady who lived within walking distance of the school. The woman was in poor health and appreciated having Sheila as a boarder, as she also helped with shopping and by performing various chores around the house.

One morning as Sheila readied herself for school, she noticed that the old woman was still in bed and complaining of not feeling well. Sheila was prepared to send for the doctor, but the old woman simply asked for a cup of tea. She told Sheila she was sure she'd feel better later. Reluctantly, Sheila left for her short walk to the schoolhouse.

It was a late autumn day, and to reach the school, Sheila had to walk through a short path that was cut into woodlands that opened upon a clearing where stood the school. As Sheila neared this opening, she was startled as she suddenly saw what looked to be the old woman literally gliding by about a foot off the ground, directly in front of her, her focus straight ahead.

In a panic, Sheila rushed back to the house. She ran inside and headed straight to the bedroom where the old woman was lying very still in bed, right where Sheila had left her. As Sheila tentatively approached the bedside, the old woman's eyes flashed open, and she lifted her head. With a wicked grin, she said, "Scared you, didn't I?" With that, her head dropped back to the pillow, and she died.

THE SHADOW BAT FROM HELL

Joseph S. Peters

Student

Houston, Texas, 1996/1997

The most frightening experience a child could go through happened to me when I was 4 years old. At the time, I was living with my mother in an apartment that seemed to exist between our realm and a much more frightening dimension. One night, I awoke to find a shadow creature perched at the end of my bed. I stood up in shock while my brain was trying to comprehend the beast that was staring me down. It was blacker than night, with the appearance of a cross between a vulture and a bat.

This shadow creature spread out its wings with a span of four to five feet, as it cried a psychic screech. The sound was so loud and terrifying that I had tears fall from my eyes before I fainted. I woke up some time later and noticed that the sliding door to the closet in front of me was open. On the top shelf in the corner stood the same demonic creature. I jumped up fearing for my life, begging the creature not to scream that awful sound. I was scared by its screech and was willing to do anything not to hear it again.

The shadow beast then flew out of my closet toward me, ultimately paralyzing my body. I could only think this was the end, for surely this bat from hell would kill me. Then in a split second, it turned around and flew through the door going out in the hallway.

Once it was gone, I regained control over my body, and I screamed out at the top of my lungs for my mother, who was sleeping next to me. She woke up and asked me what the problem was. Not knowing how to describe my experience, I told her something was in the house and that it was trying to get me! My mother immediately looked through every room to find the intruder and returned to the bed saying there was nothing in the apartment.

This was not the first paranormal event to happen in that apartment, nor would it be the last. As for the shadow creature, I can only assume it was a demon from hell. However, why it appeared to me I would never know, for we left that place long before we could find that out.

THE TOUR OF LIGHTS

H. Diskin

Machine Operator

Manchester, England, Mid-1990s

I had lived in Manchester, England for 20 years when a series of burglaries occurred in the area. It was winter time, and those bent on this crime had ample opportunity to get away with their crimes in the dark streets. As a result of this, I was very vigilant and security-conscious.

One evening when I was closing the bedroom curtains, I saw something I thought was suspicious. Across the street, I noticed the small, slim figure of a man in dark clothes walk up the driveway of a house. I hid behind the curtain to observe more closely, as I felt he was up to no good. Then something most peculiar happened. His form entirely blocked the light coming from the small window at the top of the door. I began to feel very uneasy as, in order to do this, he would have had to have been about 7 feet tall and very wide in girth!

In spite of my misgivings about what I was seeing, I managed to keep calm and remained in a concealed position behind the curtain. The man seemed to have knocked on the door and was presumably waiting for an answer. Although I was aware of the discrepancy regarding his height and the much shorter stature of the figure I had seen enter the driveway in the first place, I was more concerned that he was going to break into the house.

But then everything changed in a most dramatic way; the man altered, and the only way I can describe what happened next is that his form changed into a black, amorphous shape. He, or "it," moved away from the door like an airborne black length of material on the wind. It drifted through a solid fence and into the garden of the property next door. The entity seemed attracted to light, and as it went by each lit window, it had the ability to completely blacken the light out in a way that is quite difficult to describe. Finally, on its bizarre course, it went behind a bush and thereafter, beyond my field of vision. I presume it traveled onward into the next property's grounds.

What the entity was and why it undertook the apparent "tour of lights," I do not know. This is something I would love to know the answer to, but doubt that I ever will.

GRANDPA JACK

Reese Almack

Information Technology Computer Support

Weatherford, Oklahoma, 2009

My wife had left for the morning. I was working nights and went back to sleep. After about an hour, something woke me up. I was beyond scared; this was the most intense fear I had ever felt in my entire life. I was on my side, but knew that someone was standing at my back. I just knew someone was there. It's cliché, but the hair on my neck was tingling. My first thought was robbery.

"Pssst." The tone was clear and I recognized it. I knew that voice. This happened five days after my grandpa Jack had died. I knew it was him, but I couldn't bring myself to turn over though. We were close, but I was too afraid to look.

I don't regret not looking back, but I still wonder what this meant.

THE WALKER

Ted Bourque

Nurse

Dallas, Texas, 1990

I was going to bed for the night, so I turned out the light and closed the door to my bedroom. The room was pitch black. I got into bed, crawled under the blankets, and closed my eyes. That's when I heard someone walking around in my room.

Although I had carpet, the footsteps were very audible. The "walker" seemed to be around the foot of my bed, pacing. I got out of bed and turned the light on thinking I somehow had let the dog in my room. There was nothing there! I turned the light out and got back into bed.

Soon the footsteps started again around the foot of my bed. Then I heard them come around to the head of my bed and stop. I could feel the "walker" staring down at me. I was terrified. Before I could think of what to do, the blankets were pulled off of me. I freaked out, jumped out of bed, and turned the light on. Nothing was visibly there.

RAGE

Michael Rene Gomez

Federal Security Officer

Spokane, Washington, 2010

It was the winter of 2010, and I was in my bedroom sleeping. It was the middle of the night and the only light in the room was the moonlight shining through the bedroom window. I was lying in bed asleep with my cat beside me, when it started hissing. I instantly woke up and saw the cat's hiss was directed at the air above us.

My gaze followed the cat's to a point where I observed a form roughly shaped like the upper torso and head of a man. I had the vague impression that this entity's head was hooded. The entire entity was darker than the surrounding darkness in the room, yet the thing was still somehow translucent. The most noticeable features of this entity were the bright, glowing red eyes. The cat continued to hiss while this thing was hovering above my waistline looking down at me.

The instant that my eyes met the glowing, red eyes of this entity above me, I sensed pure hatred directed at me emanating from it. There was an instantaneous sensation of 100-percent malevolence. This entity hated me with all of its might and wanted nothing less than everything bad in the world upon me. It was at this point that I lost my temper, and I, in turn, felt burning, seething hatred for this entity with every facet of my being. The rage had taken control of me and was overpowering the sensation of hatred and malevolence that this thing was directing at me. All I wanted to do was attack, and smash, and rip, and tear, and bite into whatever flesh this thing may have had. I wanted to see and sense the pain and the fear that I inflicted before I finally killed it.

I sat up in my bed so that my face was no more than a couple of inches away from the thing's face. I was staring directly into the red void of this entity's eyes. There was no humanity there. There was nothing that resembled empathy or pity, only what I can begin to describe as a feeling of ancient, eternal enmity. It was at this point that the entity began hovering backward and away from my face. As this thing was moving away from me, I reached out and attempted to grab it with my left hand a couple of times in rapid succession, followed by my throwing multiple left hooks. There was no physical contact whatsoever. Each and every time that I attempted to physically assault this thing, my hand and my fist passed directly through the entity's head, face, and eyes without any resistance.

The entity continued to hover away from me and toward the far, upper corner of the room. I remember seeing the moonlight cast on the right side of this thing's head and torso as it passed through the bedroom. I won't ever forget the moonlight reflecting off of this thing's translucent form. As soon as this thing was out of my reach, the rage subsided and human rationalization began to return to me. It was then that this entity began to slowly phase out of sight, and for the first time during the encounter I began to feel fear. It became apparent that this entity somehow sensed the growing fear within me when I saw it look down and smile at me. The moment the entity reached the upper corner of the bedroom, it disappeared from sight. Although I could no longer see this thing, I still sensed its presence in the room, and without a definite target to channel my anger on, I began to feel a level of fear that I'd never experienced before. After looking around the bedroom trying to locate the thing to focus my hatred on it, I gave up and I starting praying. It was after praying for a while that I could no longer sense this entity's presence.

After this encounter, I spent more than two years obsessed to the point where I would search while on duty during my usual night-shift patrol. I was constantly looking through dark windows, and in darkened areas of trees and courtyards in search of two glowing eyes to lash out against one more time. I've never seen this entity again.

I've been left with many unanswered questions. The only certainty that I have is how this entity regards me. This thing sees me as prey, considers me as cattle. This entity thinks of me as an enemy, and now it will have me as an enemy until the end of time.

MIDNIGHT CALLER

Joan Rudzinski

Police Officer

Philadelphia, Pennsylvania, 2006

I'm a single mom, and one night I worked until 11:30 p.m. By the time I got home, let the puppy out, and made my way upstairs, it was just about midnight. I passed by my son's bedroom, and stopped to peek in and blow him a kiss while he's sleeping. I've done the same thing every night for 17 years.

I had two home phones in my house, one in my bedroom and one in the kitchen, though we also both have cell phones. This particular night, as I passed my son's room, I heard his cell phone ring. I listened for a minute. He didn't answer and it stopped. I didn't think anything more of it and went to bed.

The next morning I was having coffee when my son came downstairs, getting ready to leave for school, and asked, "Mom did you call me last night?" I said no, but explained that I had heard his phone ring. He showed me his phone which said our home phone had called him at midnight.

SHE WORE A FANCY DRESS

David Tracy

Entrepreneur

West Branch, Michigan, 1992

I was living with a woman friend and walked past a bay window in her living room. Out of the corner of my eye, I saw an old woman sitting outside at her patio table. When I tried to look directly at her she was gone.

I told my friend about it, and she asked me to describe the old woman. I told her she wore a fancy dress with flowers on it, with lace along the edges. She was wearing a broach and had her greyish-white hair in a bun. My friend smiled, let out a little chuckle then got up and a few minutes later came back with a picture. When she showed it to me, goose bumps shot over my body. It was the old woman, her mother, just as I described!

A GAME OF HIDE AND SEEK

Christopher Anthony

Industrial Maintenance Mechanic

Fresno, California, 1972

When I was 9 years old, my two brothers and I were playing hide and seek. We were outside with our parents, and they were doing yard work. Because nobody was in the house, I figured that would be the best place to hide, so I ran inside and vanished into the living room closet.

As I was standing in the very back corner, I felt something hit my leg. I wondered what I had knocked over, so I turned on the light but nothing was there. The area around me was clear, so I didn't think much about it and turned the light off and went back to the very back corner.

Suddenly a large hand grabbed my ankle and pinned it against the corner. My stomach was in my throat. I opened the door and grabbed onto the door jams. I had one leg out and the other being pulled into the corner of the closet. I looked to see what had me, but I was only able to see half of my leg as the rest was in complete darkness. Finally I managed to break free!

I ran across the street and sat on the curb, staring at the house. At that moment, it occurred to me that if it was the devil I had encountered, this meant he was real. This initially scary epiphany, however, meant that God was real too.

NIGHT SHIFT TERROR

C. James

Border Patrol Agent

Webb County, Texas, 1989

Twenty-five years ago, I was a newly hired border patrol agent. We were shorthanded all the time, so the new guys worked with newer guys, hopefully without making too many mistakes.

One midnight shift, my partner and I were assigned "down river." There were only four agents working that shift, so we drove around trying to do our jobs without the benefit of too much experience to hold us back. We could see a fire down near the river in an area we called the "party house"; it was an abandoned house that had never been finished being built. This made it a popular place for people to go and drink.

We turned off the car's lights so that we could sneak up on whomever was down there, as there might have been drug dealers or smugglers. We drove into the area very quietly and in near total darkness. As we rounded the last corner near the party house, we saw 15 to 20 people, all wearing long dark robes. They were standing in a circle, hands in the air, with a giant bonfire in the center.

When they finally heard us driving on the gravel, two or three members turned and started running toward us. They didn't appear armed, but they certainly were not friendly-looking either. I hit the brakes, looked around, and didn't see anything blatantly illegal going on—just crazy, nightmare, horror movie stuff. I threw the car into reverse and floored it. We shot backward, rounded a corner while going way too fast, and made it to the pavement without any lights. My partner was yelling, "Go, go, go!" and I was.

Once we were out on the highway and felt somewhat safer, I stopped to evaluate our options. Should we call for back up? Who would we call because we were basically on our own? We could call the sheriff's office. There was only one deputy working and he was far away. We could call highway patrol, but the issue wasn't on the highway, and what would we say? "Help! We're being chased by a bunch of crazies in dark cloaks!"

My partner and I were both little more than trainees, but we drove around the rest of the night trying to come up with a plan or solution for this predicament. As the sun began to rise, we decided that we would not say a word about what had happened to anyone. Our coworkers would think we were both nuts; we thought we were nuts!

The next night I snuck out there just to be sure I didn't dream it all up. I found the remains of the bonfire and foot prints. There were not any dead bodies so I felt okay about having run away the night before.

My partner went on to a different job.

THE RIVER'S EDGE

Sunbaked Droner

Student/Musician

Mexico City, 2011

There is a mystical, black-water river called the Mixcoac in Mexico City. The river flows from the far side of the metropolitan area, from southwest to southeast, and as you leave the city, it is lined with cliffs and forgotten cities. These forgotten cities are hundreds of years old, littered with wells, caves, and stone bridges. The river isn't far from main avenues, but is hidden in a surreal way; one moment you're walking on a quiet residential street, and the next you're walking through a lost passage that leads you to the magical, forested river's edge.

There are many spine-chilling stories about the Mixcoac River whispered by the locals. The testimonials include rumors of odd, flame-like lights hovering over the area, dismembered bodies regularly found on its shores, and animals behaving strangely. My neighbors were always curious about the strange barking behavior my dogs displayed, some nights well past midnight. Some evenings, all of the neighborhood dogs would howl desperately, creating an insane chorus. At first, I thought they were communicating amongst themselves, but then I realized something I wish I hadn't: that they were howling at "something" rather than each other. I was so intrigued by this oddity that I researched further into the history of the river. By speaking to elders, I found out that there was a school on one bank that used to be a mental asylum renowned for its cruelty. Across the river from the asylum, the locals practiced witchcraft—more precisely, black magic.

I spoke to my girlfriend and told her about the information I was gathering. She began to assist in my research and interviewed a local that told her a story that occurred about 30 years ago. Someone had reported hearing strange sobs along the river's edge, so the children began hanging out all hours of the night with hopes of hearing the heart-wrenching phenomenon. One night, just past 2 a.m., a group of children ran, screaming for their lives from the riverbank. This story weighed on my mind, and I thought about it and imagined what those children had experienced. What I imagined was not as sinister as the reality.

Late one night, I left my girlfriend's house on the other side of the river, which meant I'd have to cross it to get home. The moon was shining very brightly, spreading a silver haunting haze which was almost hypnotic. The road was quiet, but I naïvely decided to take a shortcut that meandered along the river's edge. Suddenly I felt that something was very horribly wrong; the panic I felt in my stomach grew greater with every step. The sensation of someone watching me was inescapable, but I couldn't tell where, so I moved faster. The faster I moved, the closer it felt. Suddenly in seconds,

I was freezing cold and it was as if I was in a vacuum without a single sound to be heard. The wind started to blow distantly and then closer...closer...CLOSER.... Only then I knew it wasn't just the wind. It was a sob so horrifying that there is no way it emanated from a human or beast. I have no idea how I managed to keep walking while the sob continued for what seemed to be an eternity. I couldn't bring myself to look behind me. Maybe if I had, I wouldn't be here to tell you this story. Finally the blood-curdling noise stopped, and I am forever changed from the experience.

Perhaps you now think I'm delusional. What I am sure of is that I was neither the first, nor the last to have such an experience on the shores of the Mixcoac River. Why should this matter at all? Let's just say that sometimes, late at night, my dogs remind me why.

THEY WERE NEVER THE SAME AGAIN

John J. Stanga, Jr.

Mechanical Designer

Bridgewater, Massachusetts, April 24, 1980

This incident took place in the very early hours of April 24, 1980, in Bridgewater, Massachusetts, a highly paranormal area. Three guys my sisters went to college with lived off campus in a rented home and had an event happen to them that would change their lives forever.

As the three boys slept in their respective rooms, there was a loud crash and one of the boys felt a body come crashing down on top of him. At first he thought it was one or both of his roommates fooling around and tried to push them off of him and told them to stop messing around. He opened his eyes and realized it wasn't them; he went into a complete panic. He was scared to death and started to scream uncontrollably.

At this time, both of his roommates heard his pleas for help and ran to his aid. When they turned on the light to his room, they were faced with a charred body lying on top of their friend. This made them as scared and panicked as their friend on whom the burnt corpse rested. They said they could actually smell the burned flesh and that it looked like the body was wearing a flight suit. The boys thought it could have been a pilot from the nearby South Weymouth Naval Air Station who had ejected from an aircraft. Suddenly the body disappeared in front of them. This completely terrified them and they couldn't sleep.

The next morning while watching the news, they saw that there was a failed rescue attempt of the American hostages in Tehran, Iran (Operation Eagle Claw). There were 8 airmen that burned to death that morning when a helicopter and a transport plane collided in the desert. This really freaked them out. My sisters said the boys couldn't wait to move out of that house; they were truly terrified. This incident scarred them and all three were never the same again.

THE EYEBALL IN MY POCKET

Michael Melvin Adams

Fitter/Foreman

Alabama, 1973

Not long after moving to Irvington, Alabama, my cousin Tommy and I went exploring in the woods behind my house. We walked up to a clearing and saw an old house with a tin roof and an old rocking chair sitting on the front porch. I told Tommy we should check it out. We were only a few feet away from the open field, but as we made our way through the brush, to the field, the old house had disappeared! We ran back and told our parents but they didn't believe us. At that time, I was 12 and Tommy was 10.

A couple of months later, I met up with my friend Bubba to walk to another friend's horse barn where she tended to her horse every Saturday morning. As we were walking, I kept feeling something rubbing on my leg between the pocket of my pants and my leg. I stopped, reached in my pocket, and pulled out what looked and felt like a real human eyeball! I screamed, my friend Bubba screamed, I threw it on the ground and stomped on it. We ran. I finally stopped and told Bubba we should go back and have another look. When we returned to the spot where the shoe marks were, the spot where I had squished the eyeball...the eyeball was gone. I told Bubba to never tell anyone about this strange occurrence.

Sometime in the mid-90s, my cousin Tommy committed suicide and Bubba was hit and killed by a car walking home one night. Maybe I am next....

THE FIGHTING IRISH

Eileen Sheehan

Certified Nursing Assistant

Dublin, Ireland, 1992

In the summer of 1992, I went to Ireland as a summer missionary on behalf of a large American Christian denomination which had an established church in Dublin. Another woman who was from Chicago was also there as a missionary. She and I were renting a room together from an unmarried Irish woman who was a long-standing member of the Dublin church. She lived alone in a typical Dublin row home found in the suburb of Clonsilla, and our rented room had two twin beds side by side against one wall with a small footpath between them.

I went to bed early one night, and as I drifted off to sleep, the Chicago woman stayed up late on her bed, sorting through her luggage. Later that night, my sleep was interrupted, as I sensed someone between our beds, standing beside me, staring down at me. I lay there quietly with my eyes closed, assuming that it had to be my Chicago roommate. Surprisingly, whoever it was punched their fist quite forcefully down, into the side of my head! In pain, I screamed out, and as I raised my hand to my aching head, I was sure that I had blood running down the side of it.

The Irish woman who owned the house had been asleep in her own bedroom across the hallway. She had heard my scream, so she came racing in to the rented room. The Chicago woman had been downstairs in the sitting room. She also came tearing into the room, but was several seconds later than the Irish woman. The Irish woman immediately snapped on the lights and ran to my bedside and shook me awake.

As I awoke, I realized I had screamed in my sleep and that there was no blood. I instantly felt very embarrassed for having voiced such a truly over-the-top scream for what had to have been a mere dream. I told the two of them what I had imagined, and also about my being convinced that the punch resulted in blood. I told them my head still hurt a little from the phantom pains of the punch which obviously never happened.

But then, the Irish woman said, "No! Something did happen!" She told us about how she also had been disturbed in her sleep. She said that about two minutes before I screamed, she had been asleep on her queen-sized bed, alone in the darkness of her room, when she woke up for no apparent reason. As she laid there awake in the dark for a few moments, she felt the corner of her mattress sprung up, as if someone had been sitting on the corner of the bed while she slept. The Irish woman's first impression of the situation in her unlit bedroom was that an intruder had broken into her home and she was going to be attacked. She immediately stiffened from head to toe in fear, when she felt her bed move, terrified she was about to get raped or murdered. She admitted that she almost screamed, but managed to stifle that instinct and pretended she was still asleep for a few more moments. That was when she heard me scream in the next room and bolted out of her bed to my rescue.

This was when the Chicago woman spoke up. She said, "I sensed something too! Let me go and get my diary! I left it downstairs!" It turned out that the Chicago woman had stayed up late to write her daily journal entries. She ran down the stairs, snatched her diary, and returned with it less than a minute later. She showed us what she had been writing up until the moment of my screams. Her diary entry for the day consisted of mundane stuff initially, including our castle visit earlier that day. She stated that she had taken some great photos, but then wrote, "I suddenly feel so ill. But not physically, more spiritually. I sense something very oppressive here in the house, an evil presence. I can hardly breathe. Maybe if I just pray it will go away." And then her writing trailed off because that was exactly when I screamed, and when she dropped her diary and ran upstairs to me.

The three of us never discussed this occurrence again through the remainder of the summer. We pushed it aside as if it never happened. When the summer ended we all went our separate ways and have never seen or heard from each other again. I remain convinced to this day that it was not a dream that violently awoke me that night. I believe that there was definitely an intelligent, paranormal entity present that night, and for whatever reason, it did indeed punch me in the side of my head. The "who" and the "why" of it remain a mystery to this day. But I maintain, without a doubt, that it did happen.

INSTANTLY THERE, INSTANTLY GONE

Janet M. Olson

Retired

Saint Paul, Minnesota, 1992

My cat, Smokey, died suddenly on April 5, 1990. Smokey was beautiful; he was part Siamese and part tabby. He had the beautiful blue eyes and the voice of the Siamese, and was always by the door waiting when I came home from work. The routine would proceed with him following me into the bedroom to change out of my work clothes. The day Smokey died was the same as always with him following me around. He was very playful even at age 13, so I had given him a bag to play with the previous evening. Suddenly, he jumped off of my bed and went into the living room. I heard the bag rattling and thought it unusual, so I went to check on him. Smokey had collapsed and died next to the bag. I was shocked because it had happened so fast. We buried him in my mother's backyard.

April 5, 1992, arrived and I was thinking about Smokey and couldn't believe it had been two years since his death. I missed him. Around 1:00 a.m., I laid in bed and started coughing as if I was getting a cold. I got up because I didn't want to wake up my significant other. I found my current cat sleeping on the bed in the other bedroom. I sat on our La-Z-Boy rocker and figured I could sleep in the chair. As I sat in the chair, I realized there was a cat in the hallway looking at me. I knew it wasn't the cat from the bedroom and couldn't believe what I was seeing; it was Smokey! He was in a light that was bright but soft. He came and jumped up on the chair, walked across my lap, and laid down by my right side. (He always did this when he was alive.) I could feel his weight, and when I reached to pet him through the light, I could feel his body. I had a feeling that is difficult to describe; it was pure love, comfort, happiness, and disbelief. This encounter lasted for about four minutes, and when he jumped down, I didn't want him to go. He disappeared. Instantly there, instantly gone.

GRANDPA'S KEYS

Joe H.

Legal

Canton, Ohio, 1986

My grandfather passed away in the mid-1980s. We sold his vehicle as we were selling some of his possessions. My mother and grandmother signed the title and the new owner came to pick up the vehicle. They could not find the car keys anywhere. The house was searched from top to bottom—in drawers and closets, on shelves and tables. They were nowhere to be found.

A few days later, my mother arrived at my grandma's house and found her to be distraught. My mother asked what was wrong, and she would only reply that she had found the keys. My mother was happy to hear the news and asked where they had been. My grandmother replied, "On the floor, in the middle of the bathroom."

We certainly would have found them quickly if they'd have been there days earlier! It seemed like Grandpa didn't want to sell the car!

WHAT DARK CREATURE

Brendan Verville

Student

Highlands Ranch, Colorado, February 2013

In February of 2013, in a sleepy suburb in Denver, my old high school friend Phil stayed at my house. Phil had been kicked out of his parents' house. He was jobless and penniless, and didn't have a car. He had no money for food, so he had been starving before moving in with me; slowly wasting away. I could sense he had suffered a deep hurt I couldn't begin to heal, but at least I could provide him a calm, clean environment with a full fridge, if only for a few weeks.

At this time, Phil and I were meditating a lot, hours at a time, and we spent our days experimenting with our own thoughts. We both agreed that it was becoming easier to clear our minds of all the clutter and focus on the meditation. One night, I turned on the TV and came across the movie *Contact*, which neither of us had seen, so we watched it. It was about human contact with alien civilizations through means of consciousness and thought. As I went to sleep that night, with Phil sleeping in the room next door, I meditated on the power of consciousness and what other worlds I could reach through intention alone. It almost seemed scary to know that my thoughts could attract the attention of other beings, and I wondered if I could make contact by simply thinking about them.

The next morning I met Phil in the kitchen. He hadn't gotten a lot of sleep, looked pale, and was silent. Finally he told me that last night he'd heard the most alien noises outside my house, somewhere near the driveway. I hadn't heard anything, as I had been fast asleep. He described the sound as something he had never heard before, a strange, guttural, choking, howling noise, which repeated itself again and again in the same pattern. He was too afraid to look outside the window, but the noise eventually stopped. I tried to come up with a rational explanation for it, but he knew it wasn't an animal because the choking had sounded almost human. Perhaps it had been a sick person coughing outside, but this thing had stayed by my driveway for at least 30 minutes repeating the same call with expert precision and strength. When I asked him if he could imitate the call, he said there was no way he could. I thought if I would have heard it, I would have looked out the window; I wondered what dark creature I might have seen. Phil admitted that his greatest fear was to look out and see a copy of himself or me out there in the street, staring back at him. That sent a chill through me because I agreed.

I believe only he was meant to hear that noise and I think it was his own way of facing his demons. Recently I spoke with Phil, who was living with a roommate. He had two jobs and seemed to be doing much better. I think he faced his dark side that night, felt the helpless despair, and now has overcome it. Hopefully he'll never confront that being again, and because it visited my house, I can only hope it stays away.

SPIRITUAL RESUSCITATION

Brandon Wayne Hitt

College Student

Longview, Texas, December 2009

In the winter of 2009, sometime in early December, I was in my bedroom when I woke up from a deep sleep. I was oddly more awake than usual, and I felt a strange presence to my left. When I turned over and looked, there was a being standing in front of my dresser. We made brief eye contact right before he reached out toward me, which resulted in my becoming fully paralyzed. My back slightly lifted off my bed, probably no more than an inch, and I had no control over any aspect of my body except for my thinking. I could barely see out of my right eye though I was able to observe a beam of light being pressed into my chest with extreme pressure. I felt no physical pain. The only thing I could feel was an overwhelming emotion or energy of love, far more intense than the love I've felt from humans. Suddenly the being left and I lay there trying to process what happened. I gathered my courage and stood up; I turned the lights on and pushed my tall dresser in front of my window. I didn't sleep for days.

I've spent years researching ancient history and studying world religions. In the past few years, I have been able to psychically channel with the being that visited me, though I've yet to experience an actual abduction. I view what happened to me as some sort of divine surgery or spiritual resuscitation. I've recently been able to rehabilitate myself from all the anxiety this event has caused me, and I'm still struggling with post traumatic stress disorder (PTSD). In recent years, I've discovered many things that have helped me understand what happened to me, but I'm still searching for answers.

SOMETHING STARING IN THE WINDOW

Steve Williams

Retired

Dowagiac, Michigan, 1957 or 1958

It was the fall of 1957 or 1958, and I was at my friend Timmy's house across the street. He always had the latest and best toys to play with. We were in the basement playing what can best be described as a child's version of a pinball machine and had been down there for some time.

It was getting dark outside, and the time was nearing for me to go home. We turned to go upstairs, when we noticed there was something staring in the window at the other end of the basement. Whatever it was, was hideous and ugly, like an old witch or an ogre. Its face had a pale, greenish tint, almost luminous in a way. We both screamed at the top of our lungs and moved as fast as we possibly could up the stairs.

At the top of the stairs was the door leading to the backyard, which also looked down a side street. When we got to the top of the stairs, we looked out of the back-door window. Down the street, we could see a dark figure that appeared to be wearing a cape or robe. When it walked beneath a street lamp, more clothing details became apparent; it was wearing a flowing garment.

What we soon became aware of was so chilling we started screaming again, this time with even more conviction. The thing that we were watching had no legs. It was floating, and this aspect was clearly visible under the lights. The only thing Timmy and I could do was just stand there frozen in place and scream. By the time Timmy's parents found us, we could hardly talk. Of course when we told them what we had seen, they looked outside but there was nothing to see. It was gone. Timmy and I never spoke about that night again.

LONG, CREEPY, BONEY FINGERS

Kelly James

Glenn, California, 2001

I was a high school sophomore when I was asleep in my room, and at 4:34 a.m., I woke up. I quickly realized I was completely paralyzed. There was a tall, male figure standing in the corner of my room across from me, and intense fear washed over my body. My room was completely black, but this silhouette radiated an even deeper color than black. His presence was terrifying. I couldn't yell for help.

He came to the side of my bed, and I could now see some details of his physique; ribs were sticking out of his torso, and his whole body looked like dark, swirling smoke. He wrapped his hands around my neck and began to choke me. He was squeezing so hard, I was panicking and believing I was about to die. Just as I felt I was about to slip away, he vanished and I was no longer paralyzed. I gasped for air, jumped out of bed, turned on the lights, and ran to my brother's room. I told him there had been something in my room, and he could see that I was obviously terrified. He searched the whole house for me and found nothing. I was so confused.

After what happened, I couldn't go back to bed so I stayed up and got ready for school. I tried to brush off what happened as a horrible nightmare. I went to school and grabbed some books from my locker. My best friend came up to me and, rather than saying hi, said, "Kelly!! Where did you get those bruises?!" I didn't know what she was talking about, but went to the bathroom to find a mirror. Across my neck were three very long, slender, deep purple bruises! It took almost three months for two of the bruises to fade away, and one of them never has! I still have a spot of discoloration on my neck to remind me of the tall, boney, male being that visited me.

Many people who have heard my story shake their heads and say, "It was just a night terror." But then how do you explain the bruises and permanent damage to my skin? They then say, "Well you could have choked yourself." No! My fingers are short, and the bruises were very, very long. Long, creepy, boney fingers did this to me.

HE THOUGHT IT HAD GOTTEN ME

Jonathan K. Marshall

Hotel/Tourism

Smithfield, Utah, 1989

As kids, we always heard stories around campfires about a thing called the Hill Side Growler. It was supposed to be a human/ape-like animal that lived in the foothills above our town.

I was 12 years old, it was late spring, and the snow was melting. My friend and I went to the Smithfield Golf Course to look for golf balls to sell back to the Golf Course. They were not open yet, so we hiked down a gully by one of the fairways and found a fresh dead deer. There weren't any bullet holes and its neck had been snapped in an unnatural position. I was curious, so I got closer and was examining the carcass. My friend was behind me, so I turned around to tell him to come take a look.

All of the blood had drained from his face and he took off running the opposite way, screaming and crying. I ran after him, caught up at the top of the gully, and asked why he was joking around. He had tears in his eyes and said through sobs that he thought it had gotten me. I didn't know what he was talking about. He said when I turned around to talk to him, a big, hairy arm reached out from the bushes that were nearest to me and tried to grab me. I didn't believe him and started to laugh, when all of a sudden this loud screaming roar came out from the trees in the gully. We were shaking. We heard heavy footsteps coming up the side of the ravine and glimpsed a big, brown blur running away from us on the opposite side of the ditch. We went back down and the deer was gone.

I COULD FEEL THE GROUND SHAKE

Billy Allen

Beaufort, South Carolina, 1998

I used to travel the low country area of South Carolina as a part of my job. I was visiting the ruins of the Old Sheldon Church near Beaufort one October afternoon. I had been there many times. There were many very old oak trees with large branches in the area. After wandering around the property, reading headstones and such, I headed back to my car. From somewhere behind me came the sound of a large tree limb snapping and falling to the ground. I could feel the ground shake as it landed just a few feet behind me, and I could smell the freshly exposed oak wood in the air. When I turned to look for the limb, the ground was bare. There was no downed limb anywhere in the vicinity. I then had the unpleasant and unmistakable urge to leave the grounds immediately, which I did.

I have not been back since.

THE ELECTROCONVULSIVE CREATURE

Coral Brune

Artist

Soquel, California, 2007

My friend JeAnne and I were driving on Old San Jose Road at about dusk. We were looking out the windows, reminiscing and gossiping, when we rounded a bend and something caught my eye. I saw it out of the corner of my eye and immediately jarred my neck to the right. I had to look full on at the creature. It was about four feet in height, with big, bolting, electroconvulsive eyes. It had a gnarly mouth and face that made me jolt due to the immense wave of heebie-jeebies that overcame me.

I wanted the car to move faster to get as far away from it as fast as possible. The thing stood still, looking at us.

I thought I had possibly imagined it, but then JeAnne, who was driving, said about five seconds later under her breath, "Did you see that?" I literally didn't know what to say; it was as if I couldn't speak or put words together in a logical manner. I had a weird flash of being somewhere else rather than in the car. Then it was over, and we continued our drive without speaking of it further.

THE BODY BELOW

Christopher Gianni

Information Technology

Rockland County, New York, 2010

I was hiking on a wooded trail in Harriman State Park in upstate New York. I was with a friend who, later in life, had been diagnosed with schizophrenia after a violent episode.

The White Trail at Harriman is a beautiful, scenic route deep in the woods. We had another 2 miles to go when we came upon a rope bridge about 50 feet above a craggy gorge.

We stopped in the middle of the bridge, carefully, as to not upset the balance. I looked down into the gorge and was shocked when I spotted a contorted body that had obviously fallen from the bridge to its death. The body was clad in the exact same clothing I was wearing. It was me. My face turned pale, and I looked at my hiking partner who had walked on and would not turn around. I started walking again, making my way off of the bridge when I had a strong feeling of déjà vu. This time I kept my distance from the edge and did not stop to admire the scenery.

HUMAN GUINEA PIG

Jim Coath

Customer Service

King of Prussia, Pennsylvania, 1976

I was about 17 years old at the crowded mall on the weekend. I was standing in front of a store with people walking by and a crowd of people around. Someone bumped into me as he walked by. There was something odd about the way he bumped into me, enough for me to turn and look at him. It had been a man who appeared to be around 40 years old with a strange, calculating look on his face. Something made me look at my arm where he had touched me. There was a small, white circle of gauze stuck to my arm. I smelled it, and it smelled like rubbing alcohol. I went into a bathroom and cleaned the dot off my arm. I think the man's purpose for sticking the dot to me was for whatever was on it to be absorbed into my body. I imagine I was not the only victim the strange man bumped into that day.

I'll always remember this occurrence, though will never truly be able to explain it.

THE BLACK HOLE IN THE BATHROOM

Patrick Leonard Olson

Project Coordinator

Brea, California, 2012

It was early in January 2012, when I stopped by my mother's home in Brea, California after work one night. I was excited to hang out with my brother and cousins, who were over for a visit, and we all sat around for about two hours laughing and enjoying each other's company. As the night grew long, we decided it was time to go. After some heartfelt hugs in the kitchen, my cousins left, leaving just my brother and me, as my parents were already asleep. My brother stepped outside for a moment to try and get his cat in for the night. I told him I would be back in a moment as I had to use the bathroom.

As I walked through the kitchen and the living room, and then into the hallway, I was greeted by a chill so cold, it felt as if I had stepped into a freezer. I immediately slowed down my approach to the bathroom, but I did continue, albeit concerned. As I came upon the bathroom door, it was open and the lights were off. I stood there for what felt like an eternity staring into the darkness of the bathroom, for it was darkness unlike any other I had ever seen. It was as if I was staring into a black hole or the deepest parts of space that light cannot touch. I had never been more afraid in my life; I could feel death around me. Inside this darkness, two red lights appeared, which I assumed to be eyes staring into me. I couldn't move. I was petrified. Whatever this was, it had locked onto me. I wanted to run, but I couldn't. Then, in an instant, this darkness came pouring out of the bathroom in such a rush it literally threw me up against the hallway wall.

I couldn't speak or yell. I felt a hand crushing my shoulder trying to keep me still as this darkness swirled around me like a tornado. I was in a fight for my life, and determination was my only ally; I fought to get away and I did. I broke free and ran. I ran toward the door as all I wanted to do was leave my mother's house. Just as I turned the corner into the kitchen, my brother was coming in from outside. We collided and he immediately grabbed my arms. Seeing the fear in my eyes, he knew something was wrong. I had tears streaming down my face and I could barely catch my breath. I told him that there is something in this house, that something had attacked me. He told me to calm down and that he would check it out. He went down the hallway and of course saw nothing; in fact, all he saw was an open bathroom door with the lights on.

Whether this had anything to do with the fact my mother's house is right next door to a cemetery, I'll never know.

THE SKY-WALKER

Llenflorida

Retired

Delray Beach, Florida, 2008

It was 4:30 p.m., one month before my mom passed away. We were on the fourth floor of the hospice; my sister and the director of the facility were sitting on the bed talking. I went to look out the window and looked up.

I became fixated on a black object that came into my view from behind a cloud. It wasn't a bird, as it seemed to be walking down an invisible road. As it got closer, I could see a huge body—hands or feet were not visible. I couldn't see its face, but it kept coming toward the window.

As it came closer, it looked like it was made out of solid black smoke. It had what looked like a silver cord around its arm and waist. It continued toward me and passed through the window near me. It was now in the room and stood at least 8 feet tall, with a cord crackling like a live wire. It turned toward my direction, and the best I can describe is that it was shaped like Bigfoot. It walked through the wall near me and vanished.

Since that day, I have lost 30 lbs and feel constantly drained.

BEDROOM VISITORS

Peggy G.

Newspaper Delivery

Ellsworth Air Force Base, South Dakota, 1980–1981

I was visited by my great-grandmother, Grandma Jo, who was a sweet, little Italian lady who had raised my mom and was the glue of my mom's family. Grandma Jo lived in Warren, Michigan, and had been ill. I was able to visit her in the hospital, but then my dad had to take me back to South Dakota so I wouldn't miss too much school.

The night she died, I was sleeping in my bed when the room got really cold. I woke up and Grandma Jo was sitting at the foot of my bed! She told me that she wanted to tell me good-bye, to be good, and that she loved me, but was happy to be with her beloved husband and was okay. I told her good-bye and that I loved her, and went back to sleep.

It wasn't until 30 years later when I told my mother the story. She relayed to me that she had also seen Grandma Jo that same night, but that she had started crying and asked her not to leave.

•••••

When I came back from Italy in August 1977, before continuing on to my dad's next base assignment, we visited my mom's family in Michigan. My Grandma Mary and Papa Jim took me to their friend's house to meet the family. The family had six kids of various ages that were kind of wild. They had one boy that was the same age as me but all we did was talk, so our relationship wasn't anything special. My family then moved to South Dakota and I never thought of the boy again. I awoke one night because the room got very cold, and over my wicker hanging chair, I saw the face of this boy staring at me. I pulled the sheets over my head and went back to sleep. A week later, we received a letter from my grandma with a newspaper clipping that stated the boy had died on the same day I had seen him in my room. The clipping said that he had been riding on the back of his older brother's motorcycle on a dirt road, hit a bump, and went flying off the bike into a tree and died instantly. I still have the clipping to this day and will never forget that night, though I still don't know why the boy visited me.

A FRIENDLY GAME OF CARDS

Thomas K.

Savannah, Georgia, 1990

Our neighbors were a young couple like us. I was in the same U.S. Army platoon as the husband, and we used to get together to play cards. Things started to get weird when he started telling us that his wife could see ghosts, that a young girl and an old man were always with her, and he was afraid of them. We didn't think much of it, as we assumed he was joking with us.

One Friday night, my wife and I went to their apartment to play cards. The first thing they did when we got there was open the door to the second bedroom, and the husband said, "Do you feel how cold it is in here? Look at your arm hair—it's standing up!" And it was. His wife came behind us and said, "They are both sitting on the bed." Again I blew it off, thinking the room was colder because the door had been closed. We then started playing cards in the dining room, which was attached to the living room. My wife and I sat facing the dining room. There were two speakers pointing away from us, toward the living room, about two feet high. The speaker on the right had a stack of books on top of it. After about 10 minutes of playing, we heard what sounded like a little bell. We all looked toward the living room, and to our amazement, a small bell, a few inches in size, lifted up into the air from behind the books. The decoration hovered approximately two feet above the speaker before it shot across the room, hitting the husband in the back of the head. My wife and I jumped up and ran out of the apartment, never to return.

UFO HUNTING

Don Warwick

Maricopa County, Arizona, 1982

I had been hunting at Table Mesa late one afternoon and was headed back to camp on a narrow dirt road. The road went over a berm, and on the other side, I saw a light shining up that I assumed was a truck coming toward me. I got out of its way by getting off the road. I went out into the desert, and as I waited for the vehicle to pass, I noticed the light stayed in the same place. I moved up the berm to look over it and that's when I saw the spacecraft with strange looking beings outside it. The creatures were short, three to four feet tall, with big eyes. I aimed my gun at them as they saw me, and they moved quickly back into the craft. I got down off the berm fast and as I was running through the desert I tripped on a jumping cactus; it embedded into my leg. The craft became airborne and flew toward me, stopping overhead where it hung suspended for about 15 seconds. It then accelerated very quickly, shot straight up, and was gone.

THE PHANTOM IN MOM'S PANTS

Alanna Bodman

Sculptor

Akron, Ohio, about 1996

My little sister and I didn't want to go to sleep. It was well past our bedtime, as Mom had tucked us in and kissed our foreheads goodnight quite a while before. We felt electricity in the air that made our skin prickle with gooseflesh, and we whispered about it feverishly; my sister was 5 and wanted to call Mom and I, being an older and wiser 7, convinced her that Mom would be mad that we were still awake. That was when there was a movement in the doorway that I saw and thought was Mom. But it wasn't.

There in the bedroom doorway stood Mom's black, skin-tight, 1980s-style leggings. They were filled out just as they would have been if Mom was wearing them...but she wasn't. No one was. I was startled and sat up quickly just as the pants ran away from the bedroom, swishing as the fabric rubbed together. They ran down the hallway, disappearing into the bookcase at the end. I didn't turn and look at my sister, as I was hesitant to remove my gaze from the hallway in case whatever I had seen came back.

After a few minutes of dead silence, I asked her, "Did you just see...something?" She reiterated to me exactly what I had just witnessed. After some time passed, we creeped out of the bedroom and ran down the stairs to find our mom and dad engrossed in a television program. We both snuck back to bed and never spoke of the ghostly leggings again.

WHENEVER GLENN WAS AWAY

Andrea Carder

Information Access Representative

Goulais River, Ontario, Canada, 2002

After graduating from college, my fiancé Glenn and I moved into a home north of Sault Ste Marie, Ontario, in the town of Goulais River (appropriately pronounced "goo-lee"). The house was a three-bedroom rental and the price of $350 each month couldn't have been beat; the bachelor apartment we vacated had cost almost double.

Despite being rural and lake-side, wildlife never ventured onto the property. Our three dogs were never settled, and this became frustrating. One night while watching a movie, Glenn and I paused and listened to a sudden, loud, non-stop hissing noise. He hurried into the kitchen to investigate and looked out the bay windows. I headed down the hallway to our bedroom where I found the cause. The bathroom sink was old-fashioned and had two separate faucets, one for hot water and the other for cold. Both were turned on full-blast and when I touched them to turn them off, the knobs fell off into the sink.

At a later time, my pillow vanished into thin air and has yet to rematerialize. The electrical switches would regularly change the lights and outlets they controlled. A visiting family of friends had whispers of "Hey" in their ears and a lamp in their bedroom turned on whilst unplugged. Needless to say, they left the next morning for the 10-hour drive home. I gave Glenn grief on a regular basis for leaving the light at the top of the stairs on, though we never ventured up there.

One incident that occurred with consistency happened whenever Glenn was away on business. The first time it happened, I was talking on the phone with him when he inquired as to whether I had our coworker and neighbor Johnny's phone number handy in case of an emergency. As I was assuring him that I did, the exterior basement doors opened and closed, and heavy footsteps made their way up the stairs toward me. I hung up on Glenn and called Johnny immediately. He drove over with his flood light and a chunk of wood with a railroad spike through it. Johnny and I scoured the house with the dogs and found nothing. From then on, whenever Glenn was away and I'd speak to him on the phone, this would happen. The dogs never reacted to the doors opening and closing or the sound of the footsteps as whatever it was approached our living area.

We lived in that house for one year before moving back to the city. We left whatever it was behind. We have never returned.

A REAL, LIVE NIGHTMARE

Anthony Valles

Student

Liberty, Missouri, 2011

I was sleeping over at my friend Sandy's place one night, watching classic horror movies with her and her mom. Freddy had just disemboweled another victim, and as I watched the viscera sloughing onto the ground yet again, I convinced them to finally turn it off. I walked into the kitchen to refresh my soda; when I returned to the sofa, Sandy and her mom were visibly excited. They asked if I wanted to go to the cemetery and try to find ghosts. I couldn't say no after having already wimped out watching the movie, so we headed out.

As we pulled into the cemetery through its massive iron gates, Sandy and I recorded every moment on our phones; it was eerie. We drove slowly through the skinny, winding roadways that were lined with graves marked by old tombstones. In the distance, silhouettes of monuments were visible in the moonlight.

As creepy as the ambiance was, the ghosts were not making themselves apparent. We parked the car and got out to stretch our legs and wander a little, still filming everything on our phones. After about half an hour, Sandy wanted to stay, but her mom wanted to go home, and I sided with her mom.

As we started to walk back to the car, a noise drew my attention to the bushes off to my left. The rustling drew Sandy and her mom's attentions as well, but I decided to look more closely. I expected to find a small animal, however a pair of large, blood-red eyes stared back at me. Whatever it was didn't blink and gutturally growled. The eyes glowed as if they emitted a light of their own. Short thick horns that had tips as sharp as pins sat on its head twisted at their tips. It lunged forward as the three of us turned and ran for our lives back to the car. We sped out of the cemetery all of the way back to Sandy's house.

When I got out of the car, I glanced at my door and was amazed to see it was slashed with what appeared to be claw marks! Was the creature really that close to catching me?! I felt sick, like this was all a horrible nightmare. Sandy, her mom, and I ran into the house and locked all the doors and windows, and huddled together to watch the videos captured on our phones. Though we didn't see the creature in the videos, we were able to hear it.

It was real—a real, live nightmare.

I'LL TAKE MY OWN CAR

Barbara J. McNey

Retired Engineering Administrator

Mountain View, California, 1970

My roommate Sharon and I were going to a party, and she was going to drive. As I got into her car I experienced a warm, time-stopping feeling from head to toe, and felt strongly that I should not get into the car with her. I also experienced a "thought-form" that told me I should take my own car, but she should go ahead in hers.

This was all very personal, so I didn't tell her why I wanted to drive separately. I was following her in my car when she crashed into the vehicle in front of her, which had stopped at a yellow light. The woman she hit was pregnant and a big lawsuit ensued. No one was hurt badly, but I would have been thrown through the windshield, as there were no seatbelts in those days. What a great lesson in trusting your intuition!

THE INVISIBLE SHADOW

Carole Krieter

Housewife

Chicago, Illinois, Mid-1950s

Our family lived in the haunted Thalia Building at 1225 W 18 Street in Chicago. Our apartment was formerly a dentist's office, and the large glass panel from the former occupants remained in the front door. We hung a shade over the glass to give my family some privacy, though any movement in the hallway cast a shadow visible through the shade.

One night, my sister and I were playing cards on the kitchen table that faced the door. We heard heavy, heavy, heavy footsteps head up the steps toward our door. The noise stopped directly in front of our door. No shadow appeared on the window shade. We sat stunned—shocked.

A long time later, the heavy footsteps moved up the next flight of stairs. The nice, sane, family man that lived up there unfortunately opened his door. We knew this is what happened because horrifying screaming began and his voice filled the hallway for a long time. Meanwhile, my mother and younger sister ran from the bedroom into the kitchen, frightened too. Shortly thereafter, the police arrived and took the screaming, (formerly) sane, family man away in a strait jacket.

1.5 MILLION SAFE MILES

Cody Joe White

Semi-Truck Driver (48 years)

Interstate 40 E, east of Harmon Den Road,
Waterville, North Carolina, 1989

Worldwide, lorry drivers tell tall tales and 95 percent of them are true. We take most with a grain of salt... which some drivers may also be transporting!

I bought and still own a SCANIA for transporting the best trees Mother Nature can grow. In 1989, I was loaded with International Veneer Company's Illinois white oak. I was headed to South Hill, Virginia, which was a 760-mile trip. The near perfect logs were individually tagged and waxed. It was 4:00 a.m. as I pulled into a rest area in Tennessee at the North Carolina line east of Waterville. There was one spot left on the end next to a grassy median. Cars on the right, lorries on the left, I pulled straight in and set the brake.

I ate some cakes with milk, and to my amazement, I perked up quickly. I noticed a lorry coming in with his lights on bright then stopping to my left behind me. I said on the CB radio, "I'm ready to leave now; you can have my spot." He said nothing so I reversed, moving 80,000 pounds 6 to 8 feet, when suddenly my lorry slammed to a stop as if we had hit a wall! I'd hit the front of a lorry that was mostly blocking the car entrance. I didn't see it pull in behind me! I got a sick feeling as I jammed the brake. The damage was done, and I had logged 1.5 million safe miles before this.

I found my flashlight and wondered if there was a long log hanging over the back end a bit. I couldn't remember. I checked and there was no overhang and there was no damage to the truck I'd just slammed! I was ecstatic; the radiator should have been in the fan, the engine shouldn't be running...but it was! I rubbed my hand over the smooth white metal. I looked for anti-freeze under the motor and didn't see any! The Caterpiller motor had its familiar sound. It was in perfect shape, and I was stunned!

The driver was in the rest area building and never came out during my wide-eyed investigation. I kept saying to myself, "What do I tell him? I've hit your lorry, but there's no damage?" To my left, a lorry rig left a space open, and I pulled left to park there. It was breaking dawn as I laid my head down over the wheel to rest and wait for him to return. It was gone when I woke up 111115 minutes later! I still think about this every day and night!

THE LIGHTNING MAN

Chris Powell

Trucker

Outside of Charlotte, North Carolina

I have thought about this all my life, but never talked about it to anyone other than once to my mom.

I was very young in my crib, and I remember what I called "The Lightning Man" coming to my window. He would talk to me, though I have no recollection of what he said. It happened many times, and once I got scared for some reason and yelled. My dad grabbed his gun and went outside; I heard a gunshot, and after that, I never saw the Lightning Man again.

Many years later, I asked my mom about what happened that night. She became serious and said, "You don't have to worry about that anymore."

About one year ago, I tried talking to her about it and she refused; she denied it ever happened and changed the subject.

A TAP ON THE SHOULDER

David Michael Sebele

Sales

Waterloo, Ontario, Canada

When I was in college, I lived in a dilapidated semi-detached house with four other guys. It was a school night, and we were all sitting around the dining room table, drinking and playing cards. The table was situated in a corner where three people would have had their backs to the wall.

It was a hot summer night and we didn't have air conditioning, so when I felt a cool breeze I became suspicious. As it passed me, I felt a tap on my left shoulder and thought someone was trying to play a trick on me. I looked to the left, saw nothing, then checked my right shoulder. When I looked to the right I saw another friend doing the same shoulder checks I just did. I asked my friend what he was looking for, and he described the exact same shoulder tap that I felt. Seeing as we were both sitting against the wall, we immediately knew it was not a trick and if not for the alcohol, we may have had a hard time sleeping that night.

SHE'LL BE BACK

Demilynn Kaneshiro

Makakilo, Hawaii, 2012

I truly did not believe in ghosts or spirits until these things happened in my home.

One late night, I was tossing and turning in my bed for hours. As the night continued, I decided to go into the living room to watch television. As I was flipping through the channels, I stopped on a station where the screen was completely red, and you could see people walking up to the camera like they were zombies. For some odd reason, I didn't change the channel, and as I continued to watch it, I started to finally doze off. It felt as if someone was watching me, though I knew everyone in the house was asleep. I lay down with no hesitation, as I was very tired, but as I was trying to fall asleep, I heard a noise in the kitchen. I quickly opened my eyes, but I didn't get up because I assumed it was my father getting up to go to work. The kitchen light didn't turn on, and I thought nothing of it. Five minutes later, I saw a little girl appear wearing a white dress that looked like it had dirt on it, and was ripped. I stared at her, confused, because I didn't have a younger sister. I looked away and looked back and in that split second she was gone. I hurried and put the sheets over my head.

Growing up, my mom always taught me not to believe in ghosts, and that if I ever felt something unholy was with me, to sing "Jesus Loves Me." I did this, and the little girl didn't reappear. I came out from underneath the blanket and saw a shadow similar to what she looked like. I saw it crawl up the wall of the hallway. "She" was now on the ceiling looking at me. Her face was dark, her hair short and black. Her head started to spin around 360 degrees. I hurried to cover my eyes again and started to cry.

I saw this girl one other time around 3:00 a.m. I got up to get a drink of water whilst experiencing another restless night. I walked up to our sliding doors where the shades had been pulled to keep the sun out in the morning. As I was drinking my water, it looked like a hand had run straight across all of the shades. There were no windows open, nor any doors. I ran into my mother's room and started crying. I'm not sure who this girl is, or what she wants, but I know she'll be back.

THE PILGRIMAGE

Ernesto Vasquez

Student

Calera Zacatecas, Mexico, 1976

During the year of 1976 in Calera, Mexico, my aunt Susana, who was 9 at the time, fell very ill, so ill that her life was in danger. My grandfather, Rafael, had prayed to the Catholic patron saint of children, that if he cured his daughter, he would conduct a pilgrimage to his cathedral in Fresnillo on foot. Fresnillo from Calera was about a two-hour walk away.

It so happened that his nephew Homero was visiting from the United States, specifically visiting his great-grandmother Tomasa. Homero had a history of drug addiction and was hoping to get away from his problems by visiting Tomasa, who was like a second mother to him.

Aunt Susana miraculously recovered, and my grandfather announced to the family that he was setting out that same night to Fresnillo. Every one tried to persuade him to wait until morning, but he felt this was the right moment to leave. It took some convincing, but the family persuaded him to allow Homero to accompany him. Homero began to say goodbye to everyone, as if he was never going to see them again, with tears in his eyes. So Rafael and Homero set off.

At around 1 a.m., after walking for an hour along an isolated road, Rafael and Homero encountered a truck coming toward them from a distance. When it was close, Homero pushed Rafael off the road and jumped in front of the truck. He was dead on impact. The truck did not stop. Rafael knew he would not be able to carry his body back, so he ran the hour back to town where he alerted the authorities. After the body was picked up, the whole family decided to wait for the right time to tell Tomasa about Homero's death, because she was old and the news could hurt her health.

That next morning, Tomasa's daughter came into the house and found Tomasa sitting on the kitchen chair. Tomasa then told her, "While you were out buying the milk, Homero came about 20 minutes ago to tell me he was going back to the U.S. and told me not to worry about him."

Tomasa died without ever knowing that her beloved great-grandchild had died that night just hours before he visited her and bid her farewell.

BEHIND THE CLOSET DOOR

John Harmon, Jr.

Lab Tech, UTC P&W

Columbus, Georgia, 1992

My children, two boys aged 7 and 10, were in Act 1 of the *Nutcracker* being performed at the Springer Opera House in Columbus, Georgia. On the night of their first dress rehearsal, we attended a Christmas Eve party at the play after the first act was finished. The children were released from supervision by the director and were told they could look around and play until their parents were ready to take them home.

It was around 9:00 p.m., and I was waiting for the children to return to the area in front of the stage. My two boys and four or five others came running to me out of breath. They told me they were looking around on the third floor and noticed a light coming from under the base of a closed door down a dark hallway. They wanted to see what was inside, so they opened the door to what turned out to be a closet. They saw a man sitting in a chair against the rear wall. He wore a white shirt with blood on it, had no feet, and stared at them with solid red eyes. All the children ran away as fast as they could to tell their parents.

My son is now 30 years old, a deputy sheriff, and if you ever ask he will tell you the same story.

SOME KIND OF TIME CHANGE

Jo Wendi Karelja

Farmer

Olympia, Washington, June 1994

I was 31 years old in 1994, attending my senior year of college. I returned to school after a failed marriage and worked at the campus radio station, hosting a three-hour show on Thursday mornings.

It was a Wednesday night in June, and I had gotten my children off to bed, so I settled down with my stereo and CD collection to prepare for my radio show the next morning. I became absorbed in the process, as I usually did when I engaged my great love of music. I suddenly realized that the time had gotten away from me and it was later than I had thought. In fact, when I looked at the clock on the stereo it read 12:17 a.m. I got up grumbling and chastised myself for not going to bed earlier, knowing I would suffer from the lack of sleep.

I went into the kitchen for a glass of water and noticed the clock on the oven read 12:18 a.m. I rolled my eyes and headed for the bedroom. Climbing into bed, I saw the clock on my nightstand as my head hit the pillow, and I cringed one more time as I resigned to my sleepless fate; it read 12:20 a.m. I closed my eyes and lay there trying to fall asleep for what I would say was at least a half an hour.

Apparently I did fall asleep, because I woke up some time later in the middle of an interesting dream which I no longer remember. What happened next I remember vividly and surely will never forget: I rolled over and opened my eyes to the clock on my nightstand, which read 11:05 p.m.! I bolted up to a sitting position while my hair stood up and my whole body had the shivers. I jumped out of bed and checked the other two clocks I had looked at earlier in the kitchen and the living room. They all read 11:05 p.m.!

The next morning as I was contemplating the weird occurrence the previous night, the phone rang. It was my friend's daughter asking if her mom was at my house having coffee with me, as she sometimes did. I said no. She paused and asked, "Was there some kind of time change last night?" The chills hit me all over again, and I had no idea what to say. I still don't!

THE THING AT THE FOOT OF THE BED

Judy Sikorski

Retired

Rossford, Ohio, 2001–2002

I was sound asleep with my husband by my side. I felt something pulling on the covers at the foot of the bed. I looked down and saw this thing that looked like a very large fish with a huge head, big bulging eyes, a humpback, and very long sharp teeth. It grabbed my foot, bit down, and began shaking my foot. I fought very hard to get my foot free but "it" wouldn't let go. I was trying to scream and wake up my husband, but I couldn't. It hurt so badly, but no matter what I did I couldn't get it off. All of a sudden it was gone, and I was awake. My heart was pounding and my foot was throbbing. No marks were apparent so I thought I imagined it.

Months later, I fell asleep on the sofa and the same thing happened again. It was terrifying! I knew just what to do; I hung a rosary on the head of the bed and stuffed another in the cushion of the couch. It has never happened again. Thank God!

SOMEONE CALLING MY NAME

Joshua Little

Oil Field Services

Dubois, Pennsylvania

My wife and I were asked to babysit her younger brother at her father's house while he was working out of state for a few weeks. We knew that her great-grandfather was either murdered or he committed suicide in the house, and that the case remained unsolved. Back when it happened, there was a trail of blood leading from the bedroom (now being occupied by my young brother-in-law) all the way out to the front porch where their great grandfather was found dead.

One night, my wife and I were sleeping in the living room when her brother came downstairs saying he heard noises in his room. Earlier that night, my wife and I got into a little argument and went to bed on bad terms. Sometime during the night, my wife shook me awake and said that she heard someone calling my name from upstairs. We sat and listened, but nothing more happened. We went back to sleep, but this time I was woken by someone upstairs saying my name. We told my father-in-law and he said that that very thing happened to him all the time...but he would hear his name. We often wonder if this is our great-grandfather trying to reach out to us.

LIKE STAR TREK, BUT WITHOUT THE SPARKLES

Jon Thies

Retired

Verona, Wisconsin, 1990

I was bow hunting deer from a deer stand 15 feet off ground which was covered in a foot of snow. Around 3:45 p.m., while looking through the trees and brush, I noticed some movement and I detected a man walking about 40 yards away. I estimated that he would pass to the right of my stand at about 30 yards distance. I looked closely at the individual and noticed he was wearing a long, old wool coat. It reminded me of pictures I had seen from the 1800s or early nineteenth century. He also wore a farmer's cap pulled down on his head and walked with determined normal steps. The man walked behind two large oaks and appeared again on the other side of them.

All of a sudden he started to fade away, much like on *Star Trek*, but without the sparkles. I could not believe what I had just seen and tried to "erase" it from my mind. People do not evaporate. I thought about it and rationalized that he must have turned and must be walking away from me, behind the two large oaks. I turned around in my stand and tried to see the man come into my view again. I didn't see him.

I got out of the tree stand and walked over to the area where I saw the man. The snow was pristine; there were no foot prints. Had I seen a ghost or witnessed a dimensional break that looked back in time?

I continue to hunt in the area, and always get up early and walk to my stand through the forest in the dark. I always fear that I may come upon the gentleman in the dark, face to face. Just in case I meet up with him, I carry a flashlight large enough to use on the front of a train.

GHOSTLY FATHERS

Pam Alexander

Registered Nurse

St. Bernard College, Cullman, Alabama, 1975

It is common knowledge among the students of Cullman College, a Catholic school, that sometimes the ghosts of priests, long since passed, can be seen wandering the campus grounds and dormitories. On the night before my graduation, my roommate Dave and I were asleep.

At 3:00 a.m., I awoke to see the door to our room wide open. While at once both deep in thought and half asleep, trying to figure out why the door was open (I knew it was closed when I went to bed), I was startled by Dave asking why the door was open. I got up, closed the door, climbed into bed, and no sooner had I pulled up my covers, than the door's deadbolt suddenly locked by itself!

I sprang from my bed, flung open the door, peered out into the hall, to find everything absolutely quiet; there was no one there. Dave had witnessed the whole thing and swore that he didn't open the door. My dog, who normally barks at any little thing, was huddled up in the corner, shivering eyes transfixed on the door. All I can figure is maybe one of our ghostly Fathers was saying his goodbyes.

BEING ON THE HILL

Rodney Street

Musician

Oakland, California, 2006

It was a very nice, clear, warm day in May 2006. I was driving to my parents' home, which was where I was raised. It was located in a suburban area with many hills and wooded areas. As I was approaching my parents' home, turning onto their road, I could see the whole bay area.

I was enjoying the view when I looked at a barren hill behind my parents' home and noticed an object on top of it. I couldn't understand what I was seeing; it had a human shape, but was much too tall to be human. I assumed that someone may have built the figure I was seeing, as after studying it, it had to stand at least 20 feet tall. I rolled down my window for a better look as I got closer, trying to identify what this thing really was. I noticed there were no birds or animals around; in fact, there was a strange, still silence.

I stopped my car in the middle of the road and got out. I was approximately 1,000 to 1,500 feet from the humanoid shape. It was solid black and had a slender body frame, but the head seemed to be slightly smaller than what would be normal human proportions and it did not reflect any sunlight. I considered that it might have been a cyclist because there is a bike route, but there was no bike and it was so very tall.

I pulled up in front of my parents' home, jumped out of the car, and ran into the street. I was perhaps 500 to 600 feet from this being. Still it appeared solid black, had no facial features, and no distinguishable clothing. No matter how close I got, it never took on a clear, defined shape; it was always slightly blurred. The being began to walk and its body shape started to distort and dematerialize. I lost sight of it as trees blocked my view of it walking down the hill. It never emerged from the trees.

A BURGLAR'S WORST ENEMY

Bart Ringer

Police Sergeant

Riverton, Wyoming, 1979–1980

One of the things that I have always liked about police work is the many opportunities it presents to follow up on hunches. Though only those hunches that seem to pan out are ever well remembered, sometimes even their fulfillment will pass well beyond the veil of any possible coincidence.

I had been working graveyard patrol for quite a while and took any and every burglary which occurred on my watch very personally. Nothing would make me grumpier than to come in to the station to begin a shift, only to find that there had been a business burglary the night before on my beat. On a number of such occasions, I had soundly chastised myself when I realized that while on patrol I had thought of checking that particular business, but had not done so.

Gradually I developed a method: If I was out driving around and thought of a particular business, I would try to come up with some reason that would have brought it to mind. If I had read a sale flyer the day before or had overheard someone talking about it, I'd ignore my hunch. On the occasions where I would draw a total blank along those lines, I would go and check the place that had sprung to mind. I started catching burglars.

Anyone who has been in law enforcement knows how rare it is to discover a burglary that is actually in progress, in a building that is not alarmed. In reality, such an encounter boils down to about 5 percent good police work and 95 percent luck. Yet in spite of those odds, I had stumbled onto six in-progress burglaries in about a two-month period, and the guys were starting to look at me sideways. As the burglaries subsided due to the subsequent lack of burglars, I shifted my efforts to finding unlocked businesses using the same methods. That year our department logged the discovery of 135 unlocked or unsecured businesses. Of them, 110 were mine and the other 14 officers on the force had accounted for the rest. The sidelong glances had continued.

I had finally come off of graveyard shifts and was working what was called a "B" or evening watch, which began at 3:00 in the afternoon and went until 11:00 at night. It had been a typically cold, Wyoming January night, and I had been in the right place at the right time and had actually witnessed a serious traffic accident. Three people ended up taking a ride to the hospital. There were four of us working that night, and as we were finishing cleaning up the intersection, I was hit with a very strong feeling that a burglary was occurring somewhere. I called the guys together, relayed my feelings to them, and asked them to go look for a burglary.

While I took a few hits as the wry cop humor kicked in, so did my reputation for being a bit "odd" along these lines. With that, they all fanned out and started looking. When our shift ended at 11:00, nothing had been found and the razzing began. With a confidence that was beginning to waver, I assured them that the night was still young and word of my "hunch" was passed on to the graveyard crew.

When I arrived for work the next afternoon, I went straight to the call box to see if there had been any burglaries. There were none. As the rest of the shift showed up, word got out and the snide comments again began to roll my way. I, better than anyone else, knew that not all of my hunches panned out, and so I took the ribbing with a sheepish smile and hit the street.

About eight that evening, dispatch radioed me and asked me to come in to the station to return a phone call. When I got back in, I was handed a slip of paper with a phone number and the name of a deputy in Lane County Oregon. I was immediately intrigued, as my mother lived in Lane County but was spending the winter in Havasu City, Arizona.

I dialed the number and got a hold of the deputy. Whenever cops talk to other cops, there seems to be an almost universal level of understanding. Even if you've never met the other guy, you will always have enough in common to talk freely and openly about anything related to law enforcement.

He told me that he had been out on patrol the night before and noticed a van which he had recognized as belonging to a local "dirt bag." He said that he had followed the vehicle for a time, hoping to see a violation of some sort so that he could stop it and talk with the driver. After a bit, with no violations having occurred, he had decided to break off and go look for something else to do. At this point, he got a little embarrassed and said, "I don't know why I did it. I didn't have any PC (probable cause) or anything, but I hit the lights and pulled him over anyways." He went on to say that one thing had led to another and as it turned out, his dirt bag driver had just committed a burglary. He had subsequently recovered a large amount of what he thought was stolen property, and in talking with the guy further, he was fairly certain that it was my mother's house that had been burglarized. She had left my number to contact in case of an emergency, and so he was calling me. He asked if I could identify any property as belonging to my mother if he described it to me over the phone, and I agreed to give it a try.

The very first item he described was an old, fancy, gold watch with a gold chain. I told him to press the top and the back cover would open, and he did so. I then asked him if it said "Luther R. Ringer Success follows striving 1893." It did, and with that, he had the verification he needed to prove the fellow he had stopped was in possession of stolen property. I asked him to mail me a copy of his report when he got it done, and he agreed to do so. I knew I was going to need it. As I hung up the phone, I took a deep breath and leaned back into my chair as the significance of what had just happened fully sunk in. The night before, at the precise time I had felt that there was a burglary being committed, my mother's house 700 miles away was being burglarized. Shortly after I had told the other guys on my shift to go out and look for a burglar, another cop, 700 miles away had, for reasons he could not explain, stopped the person who had just committed that burglary.

Later that evening at a briefing, I told the other guys what had happened. Though it was a fantastic story which was hard to believe, they couldn't imagine that I would make something like that up. There was no razzing.

About a week later, I got a copy of the burglary report from Lane County Oregon and posted it up on the bulletin board for all to see. Was all of this a coincidence? I can't imagine that it was, as the odds are just too long to explain it away like that. So what exactly was going on here? You are more than welcome to come to any conclusion you like.

Oh, by the way, I'm still getting those sidelong glances!

HER PROMISE TO BE HEARD

Khara Thompson

Podcaster

Orlando, Florida, 2012

My mom always said when she died she would be disruptive and everyone would know it.

It had been a rotten weekend for me. I was mysteriously ill to the point I wanted to call an ambulance for my exhaustion. Even worse, my apartment felt so filled with spirits, I contacted paranormal teams at midnight asking for help. I was ready to move out that very night. Around midnight, my symptoms washed away and I tried to sleep, but I felt something watching me, chilling the air. I couldn't close my eyes. Finally, when I asked it to leave, I heard bells chiming in my daughter's room. My daughter was very young though and was sleeping in her crib. I checked on her and she was fine. I then passed out in my bed from exhaustion. After two hours of sleep, I was awakened by knocking on my front door; it was the police. They explained that my mom had died in a bathtub at the exact time my symptoms were relieved and the paranormal activity kicked in. They were stunned that I was not surprised.

Since then, my mom has made dead cell phones ring and her stereo play loudly unplugged. She always sends signs to me from the other side. She has kept her promise to be heard.

BUT WHY IN VIRGINIA?

Kyle Ramsey Keatts

J. Crew Warehouse Employee

Evington, Virginia, 1997

During the summer of 1997, I was 10 years old and visiting my aunt with my dad. She lived in the woods off a small back road not far from where I lived at the time, and her yard was adjacent to a farm. My aunt had many animals; I always remembered seeing the chickens in their coop and cows out on the farm whenever I visited.

This visit wasn't out of the ordinary—not at first. Because it was summer and my aunt's house was old and had no air conditioning, it would get hot, so she always kept the front door open. The front door faced the yard which had a driveway with a lamp post. The chicken coop was off to the right of the house near the farm and woods. Around eight or nine o'clock at night, something drew me out of the house; it was an invisible force that I couldn't explain. I was compelled to go outside and look around.

When I went out, I went off the right of the house toward the darkness of the woods, right near the chicken coop. I heard something rustling softly in the leaves and twigs, crunching them. I remember hearing the leaves on bushes rustling about gently, but there wasn't any wind that night, or at least not one that would cause rustling leaves. Being a kid, I didn't know any better, and I went to investigate what I heard. I approached the thing from behind unknowingly; I won't ever forget it.

What I saw was a creature that was about my height, but was crouched down, kneeling, doing something I couldn't see as it was too dark. What I could see has haunted me. I saw huge, oval shaped eyes, with pupils that slowly focused on me as it turned its head. The creature's eyes were red and glowing with black, sharp, thin, cat-like pupils. I could only stand there as I was literally frozen. I was right next to it, maybe a foot or two away, if that. I couldn't move or yell for help. I was paralyzed by the fear from what I was seeing. This lasted for what I believe was less than 10 seconds, but it felt like forever.

When I could move, I ran for my life, about 25 maybe 30 feet to the front porch. I got my dad and showed him what I saw, but the thing was already running away with strides similar to a hopping kangaroo. Its legs were bent inward, but it was very fast. This thing looked grayish-green with quills on its back, or spikes, or something similar. This creature was strange to say the least, but from what I know of cryptozoology I want to call it a chupacabra. I know it's weird, but why in Virginia?

I wish this was the end of the story, but something even more strange happened when I moved from where I lived that summer, to my other aunt's trailer on a piece of property located in Campbell County near another forest. When I lived there, I remember always sleeping on the couch in the living room as I disliked my bedroom due to the fact it was cold and uninviting. Whatever this chupacabra-like thing was, it followed me there and appeared several times at night as I tried to sleep. It would always stand and look at me from the kitchen. I never saw its body, always its eyes. I considered that it may have been my imagination, but it was odd that I kept seeing it. My fear melted away after a while; I just respected that it was a strange creature.

Finally, on my last night in Campbell County, I saw it one last time. I remember looking out the living room window and seeing a bright, white light envelop the front porch area. Once the light subsided, it was over. I no longer saw the thing in the hallway or bright lights on the porch.

I ASSUMED IT WAS MY MOTHER

Melanie Williams

Administrator

Sydney, Australia, 1980

When I was 13, our family moved into a newly built bungalow on a new estate called Woodbine in Campbelltown, a southwestern suburb of Sydney, Australia. It was on what was farmland, so it was quite remote from the town center, all new and modern. One night it was particularly hot, and I had my window open with the curtain flapping in the cool breeze. Everyone was asleep, and as I laid there, I heard a shuffling noise coming up the hallway. I assumed it was my mother, and her slippers were dragging on the carpet. I heard the shuffling come into my room and stopped.

It felt like someone was staring at me, so I sat up and said, "Mum?" I was looking up at a tall, white, human-like shape with no features but a round, white head. I went under the covers and was frozen with fear; I could hardly breathe. After a few minutes, I managed to whisper to my sister in the bedroom across from me and ran to her bed for the night. I told my parents and they tried to ease my fear, but it didn't help when the following week a photo appeared in the local paper showing a woman in a white hat working on the farm in the 1800s where we were now living.

I have never forgotten what I saw or the fear, and I still search for answers. Was it a ghost, a night terror, an alien, or my spirit guide?

WHAT THE HECK WAS THAT?

Michael Grady

Drafter/Designer

Ellis County, Texas, 1992

This encounter happened many years ago, but the image of what I saw has been seared into my mind forever.

One night, my friends and I decided to do something out of the ordinary. We wanted to explore the urban legends of the surrounding area. I got a call from my buddy, who wanted to go pick up our friend Kay and go to an old, abandoned cemetery. We had heard all kinds of stories and legends about this place, so we wanted to see if they were true. It took an hour or so of driving, some of it down a dirt road, but we found what we thought was it. There were headstones going back to the 1800s, which seemed pretty cool to teenagers like us. We tested some goofy legends, and as we suspected, nothing happened. We laughed it off and started to make our way back to my car.

That's when we heard rustling in the bushes. For a moment, we stood frozen in fear, then used a flashlight to find it was just an armadillo foraging. As we drove away, we decided to take the long way back to the city, because we all had hours before curfew.

When the dirt road turned to pavement, I thought I would have some fun; I dropped a gear and floored it, we slid sideways, then took off. I should have been paying attention, but I wasn't, and before I knew it, we got turned around. It was dark, the corn crops were high, and we were going really fast. Somehow we got off the main road and got lost. We turned down a road that was bumpy, and it was getting nerve-racking because we didn't have a map, it was late at night, and we were in the middle of nowhere. My buddy joked about *The Children of the Corn* movie, which I think scared him more than it did me and Kay.

We came to this stop sign that was in a weird spot. It was in the middle of a road that had corn on either side. No crossroad? As I stopped, I turned to Kay and Jay and asked, "So, do we go back the way we came or do we..." Before I could finish, Kay's eyes got really big and she started to shake. She mumbled, "What the heck is that, Mike?"

Jay and I both turned and, in the headlights, there was a tall creature hunched over, walking out of the corn field in front of us. It had long arms, longer than any human being I have ever seen. The hands were curled up and the finger tips looked pointed. The thing had a long snout and pointed ears. It stopped and gave us a half smile showing its teeth; they looked like monster teeth. It then turned and looked directly at us. Its eyes reflected the light from the headlights and it simply walked away. We rolled our windows up and sat there dumbfounded for a minute or two. I looked at Jay and put the car in gear. I rolled up the 10 yards or so to where the thing crossed the road. There was nothing, but more corn, an old wooden telephone pole, and an old abandoned farm house.

Kay ever so quietly said, "Mike, I want to go home. Please don't drive past that house. Let's just go." Jay agreed, so I put it in reverse and we slowly backed down the road and went back the way we had come. I looked one last time at the abandoned farmhouse in the rear view mirror in the moonlight. I saw movement just inside the open door, and it scared me so much that I had a cold feeling go through my body. I remember flooring it, causing us to bounce and jostle our way up the crappy road.

I drove a few miles, pulled over and got sick. The entire time the other two were urging me to come on and hurry up and get back in the car! We finally got back to civilization, and Jay and I dropped Kay off at her house. She leaned in the passenger-side window and said, "I don't want to talk about this ever. I have never been so scared in my life. If there are things like that out in the world then...let's just not ever bring it up. Come on guys please! Swear." She looked at both of us with tears in her eyes. We swore, and we never spoke of it again.

As Jay and I drove off, Jay stared out the window. Halfway to his house he said, "I was always told that...." He hesitated. "That monsters didn't exist. But, if they don't exist, what was that?" He turned to me and I looked at him. I could see the fear in his eyes as I'm sure he could see the fear in mine. I didn't say anything. I couldn't, because I didn't know what to say. We drove the rest of the way in silence. All I could do is think, "Monsters are real." All three of us will never forget that night as long as we live.

THE OPEN GATE

Nancy A. Ayers

Retired Healthcare Worker

Cheyenne, Wyoming, 1981

One day, as I was walking my 180-pound, half mastiff/ half Chesapeake Bay Retriever by our local cemetery, I noticed that the typically closed gate had been left open. As we walked past the open gate, my dog suddenly leapt into the air, lunging and snarling, seeming to attack something invisible to my eyes. This dog would fight the devil himself to protect me and from what I was witnessing—maybe he was!

For what seemed like an eternity, but was actually mere seconds, my dog put up the fight of his life; biting, snarling, jumping, and lunging at some invisible fiend! As I pulled with all my might to drag him away from the open gate, cars were stopping in the middle of the road to watch the struggle. When I finally got him across the street, his battle with the invisible foe stopped. Whatever the attacker was, it evidently could not follow. I never went near that gate again and have decided that fences around cemeteries are not to keep stuff out, but are instead there to keep whatever's inside in!

IT'S OKAY

Nancy Joyner-Lutz

Retired

Taylor, Michigan, 1982

With my recent divorce, I was left on my own to care for two babies and forced to go on food stamps to feed my little ones. I was so ashamed. The first time I used them, I was horrified. I sheepishly put my children in the cart and started grocery shopping. I wanted to die.

When I arrived in the dairy department, I placed a gallon of milk in the cart, then turned to reach for a dozen eggs. I saw a hand grab my wrist; it was an old hand with long, thin fingers. I followed the hand up the arm to see an old lady, perhaps in her 80s, dressed in an old black mohair coat and hat. She smiled when my eyes met hers and she said, "You are ashamed, but don't be. You must do what you need to do right now...to care for your children. Your ex will want to return to you, but don't let him. He has no place with you now. You will marry your dear friend...and you will be happy...but you will lose him.... But it's okay...you will be happy again... afterward...." Her eyes were the bluest I had ever seen. She then walked over to my children, touched my son, 6 months, on the head, and said, "It's okay...they can fix him. The doctors are wonderful now. He will be okay." Then she walked over to my daughter who was two. She touched her head and said, "This one is blessed. She is from God. She is special."

I stood there, in shock. Who was this woman? Why was she touching my children? How did she know all of my shameful secrets? Most of all, what was she talking about when she said, "He will be okay"?

She stopped talking, smiled, turned, and walked to the back of the store. I snapped out of my shock and turned my cart toward the back of the store and followed her. After all, I had questions. When I reached the back, she was gone! Now, she was at least 80 years old—how fast could she move? I went across the back of the store looking down each aisle, frantically looking for her. She would have been easy to spot in the odd old coat and hat. I never found her. She was simply gone.

In the years to come, all of the things she had told me came true. They discovered my son had a heart defect, and he had surgery to correct it. He mended perfectly, just as she had said. I also ended up marrying my best friend from college, who I would later lose in a car accident.

But who was this woman? And why did she choose me? Does God send angels to you when you are at your darkest point in life? I think so!

THE CHILDREN'S HOME

Christopher Wilkerson

Dry Cleaner

Bonham, Texas, 2002

There was an old children's home that had been built in the 1890s, close to Ladonia, Texas. The building used to be pretty big, but after so many years of neglect and lack of maintenance, it had fallen apart as any building would. By the time my crew—Nathan, Steven, Zach, and Cassie—and I got to the place, it was only a small foyer and an auditorium. The yard outside was wild and the grass had grown as tall as I was. There was still some rubble remaining from the rest of the building that had crumbled.

When we showed up, it was still daylight outside. The first thing we did was check out the property, looking around and seeing if we felt anything unusual. I really didn't feel much, a couple of cold spots but nothing to get really excited about. However, when we stepped into the building it felt different, and there was a cold wind coming from somewhere. One of the walls in the auditorium was somewhat demolished; there was a big section of the wall missing that left a large, gaping hole. This hole in the wall used to be a hallway leading to the other parts of the children's home, but all that was left was the foundation piers coming out of the ground. We figured it was just the wind we felt blowing through the hole, but the wind wasn't blowing from that direction. I followed the cold sensation all the way from the front door up to the stage, where it stopped. Now all of us couldn't feel anything but a slight breeze coming from through the big hole in the wall. We looked around a little bit more, checked on the stage, then went under it. There wasn't much there, just a couple of chairs, a podium, some tables—nothing out of the ordinary. Because we had felt a couple of anomalous cold spots earlier, we decided to come back later that night.

We returned around 10:00 p.m., got out of the car, and started walking toward the house. Steven had taught Nathan, Zach, and me a new way to ground and shield ourselves from paranormal attacks. We also learned how to turn the shielding process around so we could sense the presence of ghosts more easily; I had turned my shield into a type of ghost radar. When I stepped onto the front stairs, an icy cold sensation went down my spine. When I stopped, Stephen asked, "Did you feel that?"

"What do you think it was?" I asked in return.

"Their fear, maybe," Nathan said.

I looked up at the foyer just as a shadow passed across a hole in the back wall. When we finally gathered ourselves, we headed into the auditorium. When we walked in, I instinctively looked up, and I saw what looked like a rope hanging from one of the rafters over the stage. At the end of the rope was a dark figure, slowly swinging in small circles as if it had only been hanging there for a few minutes. We all saw it. Cassie started to go back to the car, saying she didn't feel well. We decided to leave. As we were driving away, I took one last look at the building before we pulled out. I saw what looked like maybe 10 or 15 floating balls of light suspended in mid-air where the rest of the structure once stood.

The next day, I did some research on the children's home and asked a few of the locals about its history. One of the women I talked to said she used to deliver milk there when she was younger. She said that one of the caretakers had killed most of the children and then hanged himself.

One month after this experience, I enlisted in the army. I drove by the old structure one more time a few days before I was shipped out to basic. Sadly, the only thing that was left standing was the chimney.

THE DEEP-BREATHING DEMON

Fay Sennet

Retired

Seattle, Washington, 1964

I was a recent high school graduate of 18 years old. It was summer, so it was already daylight at six in the morning. I followed my daily routine of making breakfast for my parents and sack lunches to take to their jobs. Afterward, I returned to bed as usual. I laid down on my left side facing the wall and closed my eyes. Still awake, I heard three deeply exhaled breaths behind me. I turned over, onto my back, so that I could view the room and try to locate the sound.

What I encountered was pure, frightening evil. A demon was next to my bed. It was in the shape of a cone, the height of an adult, composed of a substance that looked like grey, semi-transparent Jell-O. It had wart-like bumps the size of walnuts all over its body. It had teeth and fangs, like a dog, and slits with yellow eyes. It didn't have any arms or legs, just a conical, Christmas-tree-shaped body. It was pure evil. It rolled over on top of me, and started to dissolve into, and possess me. I said, "God please help me," and instantly it was gone. I got up and ran to my parents who were still seated at the breakfast nook. They didn't believe me. They said I had been watching too much television and reading too many books. They left for work as usual, but I didn't go back to the bedroom.

I am now shaking as I write this. However, from this experience I am able to derive the fact that the name of God alone has power over any and all evil. It is love.

MAMA'S BABIES

Colleen Barnhart

Realtor

Carlsbad, California, 2010

In the summer of 2010, my little boy Logan was around 18 months old. We were so happy to have this smart, growing little boy, as I had lost a baby at 21 weeks a year before Logan was born. I lost a second baby at 15 weeks when Logan was only 9 months. Of course, my husband and I were devastated, but so happy to have our son. Logan was so young he never knew I had lost a baby before him or during his babyhood.

One evening while I was putting him down to sleep, as I usually did, I would talk to him while he was drinking his bottle, laying him down very calmly. Out of no-where, he threw his bottle down, sat up, and started pointing to the top corner of his room right over my head saying, "Mama's babies...mama's babies." At first I thought he was just jabbering, but when he got up and moved toward the area where he was pointing, looking intently still saying "mama's babies," I started to get the chills. I know babies and small children can see things adults cannot. I knew at that point he was interacting with something I couldn't.

Years later, we had our second son, Liam. Logan has loved Liam since before he was born. I just wonder if one of those little spirits was waiting to come back and maybe Logan had met Liam that day.

WALKING AND PRAYING

E. Niles

Environmental Compliance Manager and Professional Registered Engineer

Knik, Alaska, 1997/1998

In the Knik, Alaska, area, I was walking the loop around the lake that goes through the woods, off North Shore Drive and past the local chapel. I began walking along Knik Goosebay Road. I was praying when I began to hear the loudest screaming. I stopped, looked around, and saw nothing; no cars or people and silence. When I began praying and walking again, the screaming became audible. Again I stopped praying and the screaming would stop. I walked past the entrance to the old Indian Cemetery that had spirit houses and heard screaming again. This time when I turned back, I saw an Indian man coming toward me wearing typical Alaskan clothing. He was on the trail from the cemetery. I started to pray and he started to scream. I turned toward him and saw that he did not have a face. I rebuked the spirit, and it screamed and disappeared.

STRANGE BEAST

Marc Kivisto

Casino Dealer

Menomonee Falls, Wisconsin, 1986

It was a warm summer night with clear skies in late August 1986, when my dad and I were walking our dog at about 10:00 p.m. We were on a dirt road near a large swampy nature preserve in southeastern Wisconsin. All of a sudden, something crashed in the wooded area at the side of the road and made the loudest, most unbelievable scream I have ever heard. My dad and I froze in our tracks, and the hair on my dog's back bristled. We turned and walked back the way we had come, and while we did this, whatever was in the woods decided to move parallel to us; we could hear it walking through the brush at the same pace. When we stopped, it stopped. This continued for about 200 yards until we left the road and walked across an adjacent field.

Both my dad and I are avid nature lovers, so this experience baffled both of us. Neither of us could explain what we just heard. To this day, I can't explain what native animal could have possibly made a noise like that. Also, what could walk in the pitch-dark, through thick brush, at the same speed as we were?

PAP

Gabriel Holden

Chef/Filmmaker

Baltimore, Maryland, 1979

It was the second Saturday in November, 1979, and I was up early watching cartoons. I sat in the middle of the living room when the phone started ringing over and over again. We didn't have an answering machine, and I wasn't allowed to answer the phone because I never took messages. We recently had a new number assigned because we had just moved into the apartment in which I sat. I went upstairs to get Mom, and both Mom and Dad came down. Dad started making coffee as my mom answered the phone.

It was my great-grandfather, "Pap," whose name was actually Robert. He was an old Irish guy with an accent. I remember he called me "Gabriel Heater," after a guy who was on the radio during World War II. Pap had called to tell my mom he loved her, me, my dad, and the rest of the family, and how proud he was of us all. Being the old, stoic, Irish man he was, he typically wasn't much for sentiment. My mom thought this call was a bit odd and figured the old man had worked the night shift, then threw a few drinks back afterward and was feeling sentimental. She told him how much she loved him and I joined in. She gave me the phone, and I yelled, "Love you, Pap!" He said, and I will never forget this, "I'm always here for ya, Gabriel Heater. Always." I said, "I know, Pap! See ya later," and gave the phone back to my mom. She told him goodbye and that she loved him, and then hung up.

About 35 minutes later, Mom got another call and burst into tears. The Maryland State Police called to say that Pap had died about two hours earlier in a car accident on the I-83 right outside Baltimore while driving to work. The police had found a greeting card in the car that my mother had written our new number on, and because they couldn't reach anyone else, they called us. They asked Mom to inform the family. Of course she didn't believe the officer, because we had just talked to Pap minutes before. That was until she and my grandmother went to identify the body. I clearly remember all of the conversation surrounding the event, because Irish wakes were held in the home and that call was all everyone talked about! To this day, my mom tells the story at every Thanksgiving dinner!

NIGHT FISHING AT THE DAM

Gary Lee Buchanan

Skilled Laborer

South of Lincoln, Nebraska, 1983

I went fishing and stayed out until it became really dark. I was settled into a great spot when I heard a splash that I thought was a fish jumping! I heard another splash which made me realize that it wasn't fish jumping, but rocks falling from the top of the dam, below which I was camped. It was black as pitch out, so I couldn't see anyone, except for the light of a lone, faint lantern on the other side of the lake 3 or 4 miles away. I picked up my lantern and gear, and left the camp to head toward my truck parked at the other end of the dam. A few other families were fishing with their kids earlier, but they left when the sun went down.

As I walked, rocks would continue to splash into the water from above, as though someone was following me and throwing them in the water just for me. I really thought that someone was going to attack me. When I arrived at my vehicle, I placed my gear in the bed of the pick-up on the passenger's side and began to walk around the front of the pick-up toward the driver's door. I thought to myself that if something was going to happen, it would have probably happened right then. As I approached the driver's door, it flew open and startled me, but nothing was there. Feeling a bit afraid, I continued around the door and proceeded to get in not knowing what to expect. I turned on the truck and drove away.

After many years of wondering about the experience, I came to the conclusion that it possibly was a spirit. How the door flew open, how perfect the timing was, and how there was no evidence of anyone there, tells me whatever it was, was invisible. It seemed impossible for anyone else to be there because of the location on the lake and the fact that everyone else left. When the door opened, there was no noise from the door unlatching. Whatever it was, it gave me a royal goodbye instead of a welcome. I'll definitely never forget it.

THE BACKPACKING JOURNEY

John F.

Electrical Systems Engineer

Mononagahela National Forest, West Virginia, 1992

Years ago, my wife and I went backpacking in West Virginia, near the Seneca Rocks region. After driving to the park, we had dinner at a restaurant. We were eavesdropping on the table next to us and the conversation they were having chilled us; they spoke of practicing witches in the region. After leaving the restaurant, we found a nearby camping supply store. As we returned to the car, a man came running across the street, frantically screaming, "Do you see the smoke?! Did you see the explosion from inside the store?!"

I had no idea what he was talking about, so I dashed back to my car and left. The next morning, we backpacked into the forest and made camp along the trail. Later that night, I awoke to the sounds of light raindrops tapping on our tent. In the morning, however, there was no sign of any moisture on the tent or the ground, and the sky was clear. We broke down camp and hiked further into the forest. We left the trail, deciding to follow a creek that entered into a valley with a series of beaver ponds.

As we made camp at the last of the ponds at dusk, the wind began to blow. It seemed to have an intelligence as we could hear it approaching, but it never touched us as it passed by into the bending trees. Other times it would find us. Our campfire gave us some comfort, but that comfort was broken by a short, loud scream that repeated every 10 to 15 minutes. It circled around us but did not approach us. As we went into our tent to sleep, I took one last look at a star-filled sky and grabbed my axe.

A minute after turning off the tent light, I heard the tapping sounds of raindrops that I had heard the previous night. We knew they were not raindrops now, and imagined the flicking, tapping of fingernails on the tent. I couldn't stand it any longer, so I turned on the light and the tapping stopped immediately. I took my ax and went out the tent door to see if anything was there. Nothing was seen: no rain, moisture, or clouds, only a star-filled sky overhead. After returning to the tent and extinguishing the light, it started again. We couldn't believe it. I told my wife that at least it seemed to not be trying to come inside. I held onto my ax tightly. Five minutes later it finally stopped, and I slept very lightly the rest of the night, only hearing the beavers gnawing on wood.

The next morning, as we stepped out of the tent, we were greeted by a very large bird that was waiting for us. We watched it fly down the valley toward us, then it swooped down at us. Both my wife and I dropped to our knees, feeling we were being attacked as it passed merely a few feet over our heads. It flew off and did not return. Hoping to find some clues as to the source of the screams from the night before, we hiked up the hill. Halfway up, I noticed something standing about 20 feet ahead. As I looked up in an attempt to see it more clearly, it was gone. I thought I had just seen a soldier in an old uniform. I questioned myself as to whether I really had seen something, but before I could say anything, my wife behind me excitedly asked if I had just seen the soldier in front of us! An electric chill went through me.

We continued up the hill with our eyes wide open, and as we reached the crest, I noticed a clearing. The clearing on this remote hilltop was about 150 feet in diameter and was planted with grass that was thick, overgrown to the point where it bent over due to its height and weight. At the middle of the clearing, there was a circular ring about 40 feet in diameter of young evergreen trees, each about the same height. The ring had a wide slot for entry and, within, had the same overgrown grass. At the other end of the clearing, there was a bulldozed path coming from far down the other side of the hill. We returned to our campsite and found many animal foot prints—as if they inspected it while we were up inspecting the hilltop.

Our last night camping was undisturbed except for the beavers doing their usual work.

The next morning my thoughts were of returning back home; that's when I realized what time of the year it was. My hair rose as I asked my wife whether she realized that we just spent Halloween in the creepy wilderness!

When I returned to my job, I remembered a secretary who annually visited Salem, Massachusetts on Halloween to join other witches there. I described our weird backpacking experience to her, and she responded that the hilltop was a witches' ceremonial site, that they were playing with us and our minds on Halloween. She remarked that my wife and I must have a very strong mental state to have withstood it.

Since this revelation, I always think of returning one day with more protection, friends, and a Rottweiler or two.

VISITING FRIENDS

Nadene Rocha

3D Graphic Artist

Utah, 1973

I was about 15 years old when this happened approximately 40 years ago, so some of the detail is a bit fuzzy, but I remember the important part clearly. My best friend and her family were going to take a road trip from California to Nebraska to visit my friend's sister and husband. They had moved to Nebraska a few years earlier, and I was asked to go along. There were about five of us all together, so four of us piled into the back of a little camper, on the back of a pick-up truck.

My friend's mother was the driver, so she took us through Utah to get to Nebraska. She had a friend there, so we visited for a few days before continuing on with our road trip. We were staying at an old Victorian farm house, and my friend and I slept downstairs on the sofas. There was a restroom on our level, so we had no reason to go upstairs the entire time we were there. Everyone else slept upstairs, and as far as I was concerned, the stay was uneventful.

On the day we were going to leave, we were almost finished packing up the camper when my friend's mom asked me to go upstairs and retrieve her purse from the bedroom she had slept in. I went up and found the room to be empty of furniture; there was not so much as a bed or dresser filling the empty, gaping space. I thought it was strange, but maybe she had used a sleeping bag. I went over to the window where the purse was sitting on the floor, picked it up, and looked out the window. I could see everyone downstairs crowded around the pick-up truck immediately below. I watched for a few seconds—no more than a minute—and that's when I felt a hand come down on my shoulder, as if to say hurry up. I fully expected someone from the group had come up there to get me moving. When I turned around, there was absolutely no one in the room with me or in the hallway outside the door.

It hit me at that very moment how utterly strange it all was. I had felt the fingers on the hand—it had been real! I was able to brush it off by reminding myself that I'd never be returning to this house again. I calmly but quickly walked to the stairs, went down them and out the door. We left immediately, which was perfect. If I'd had to stay another night, I would have slept in the camper.

THE SWEATY MAN

Melinda Warner

Nursing Unit Secretary

Kansas City, Missouri, 1981–1984

When I was almost 16, I got my first job as a maid at a local Holiday Inn. After you worked there for a while, you were assigned a permanent station. Mine was on the third floor of the south wing of the hotel, and I had 15 rooms to clean per day.

It was late afternoon and very quiet. Most of the guests had already checked out and I was going about my routine. I turned to see a man standing in the room. He was about 45, balding, and was wearing a white t-shirt, gray sweatpants-style shorts, and short white socks with tennis shoes. He was sweating profusely, as if he had just been for a run. He asked me if I had found a small gold ring. I told him no, but if I did I would turn it in to the front desk. He left the room. I went out into the hallway shortly thereafter, and he had disappeared. The room I was cleaning was not near an exit, but I just brushed it off and went back to work.

A few months later, I was again simply working through my stationed rooms, when I sensed someone behind me. I turned to see a man, dressed in sweaty clothes, standing in the room. I vaguely recalled his face, but when he asked about the ring again, it reminded me of the previous occurrence. I again told him if I found it I would turn it in to the front desk, and again he walked into the hallway and seemingly disappeared into thin air. This same course of events happened to me 17 times during a period of three and a half years!

The last time it happened, I was not working on my usual station. This time I was on the first floor on the north side of the building, facing the parking lot. It was summer, and as I cleaned, I looked out the window. I saw a man walking across the asphalt in bare feet; it was 100 degrees outside, and the parking lot was topped with tar. A few minutes later, I turned to see the same man in the room with me. A chill ran up my spine when I realized it was the same man from before. I hadn't seen him for at least six months. This time he carried a small canvas bag that he set on the dresser. It clanged when he set it down, which startled me. I felt fear for the first time and brushed by him to leave the room. I went to get my supervisor, but the strange, sweaty man had again vanished by the time we returned to the room.

Through the years, I thought he might be just some kind of stalker, but he always looked the same, dressed the same, and asked me the same question. It also wouldn't explain his uncanny ability to disappear into thin air.

THE CHURCH OF NIGHTMARES

Michele Brooks

Social Worker

Small Town by Ottawa, Ontario, Canada, 1995

When we were in our early 20s, some girlfriends and I went camping. We decided to drive around looking for new places to explore. At one point, I was driving when we passed by a large church located on a big hill far from the road. This was exactly when I started to have a panic attack and had to pull over. I could not explain why this happened. I told my friends we would not be driving back to camp that way.

After we returned home, my father asked how the trip was. I described all the fun things we had done and then, hesitantly, I began to describe the situation in which I experienced my extreme anxiety. He interrupted me and named the small town in which the church was located. He told me that he drove by there once and would never do so again. Of course I had to ask why, as my father is pragmatic and certainly not a superstitious man. He said as a child he had a recurring nightmare about this exact church. Oddly, he wasn't born locally; he is from Jamaica, in the West Indies.

SECURITY PATROL

Nick Bailey

Security Supervisor

Ogunquit, Maine, 2012

I arrived at the hotel around 1:00 a.m. and began my interior patrol of the facility, beginning by walking down the first floor hallway. I started to hear footsteps on the floor above me, which was odd because it was just before

Christmas, and this particular hotel had closed-down two weeks earlier. I walked up the stairs cautiously, not knowing what I would find. I checked the hallway and every room in that wing, and found nothing that would have created that noise.

I went back downstairs and continued rounds where I had left off. Again I heard footsteps coming from the second floor, but this time from the opposite end of the hall. Again I ran upstairs and checked, and again I found nothing. I figured it was an old building and it was just making noises as old buildings tend to do.

I continued my rounds and found a light out close to the end of my patrol at the far end of the first floor hall. I took out my notebook and began writing the location of the blown light, when the hair on the back of my neck and arms stood on end. I then heard a noise that sounded like someone full-on sprinting toward me down the hallway! I dropped my notebook, turned around with my fists raised...to find no one there. I grabbed my notebook and left the building.

THE ILLUMINATING DARKNESS

Paul J. Evans

Student

Virginia Beach, Virginia, 2006

I had just gone to bed and the two other people that lived in the apartment, my brother and our roommate, occupied the bedroom upstairs. I always slept in the dining room on my futon, and that night, at about 2:00 a.m., I felt a heavy sense of dread and fear fill the room. I turned over and looked into the room from the corner where my bed sat. On the other side of the wall behind me was the living room, and in front of me was the kitchen doorway. Further along the same wall was the hallway leading to the door outside.

When I looked toward the foyer, I saw a form enter into the room that was cloaked in darkness with its cowl pulled down over its face; it resembled a monk. The dark form was holding something in its right hand that looked like a lantern; its arm was raised high over its head. This lantern was pure black as well, but it glowed. The entity was in fact a contradiction, as it seemed in its entirety to be a source of light, glowing darkness. It entered the dining room where it immediately, sharply, turned right. It was coming toward me. There was a bookcase between the foyer doorway and the kitchen doorway, and a small dining room table in the middle of the room, with some boxes on the floor. It walked, gliding, through them all.

It never looked directly at me, but floated through the room, through the table, the boxes, and the bookcase. When it reached the kitchen, it went through the doorway and then vanished. When it disappeared, the sense of fear and dread immediately melted away.

I'M GOING TO REST NOW

Elizabeth Kay Amaireh

Cafeteria Manager

Oklahoma City, Oklahoma, 2003

I lived in a little house in a quiet neighborhood with my son, Daryl. Since we had moved into the house, there had been odd little noises. Things would be moved around, and sometimes I would hear my name being whispered. My son worked nights and I would be home by myself. I had seen shadows from the corner of my eye many times, but never paid much attention to them. I simply thought it was my imagination.

One night I was fast asleep when the blanket was jerked off of the bed. I sat up quickly and saw a figure standing in the doorway. I shouted out, "Daryl! What do you think you're doing?" The figure in the doorway looked back over his shoulder and said, "I'm not Daryl, I'm going to rest now." That was when I remembered Daryl was at work; I was the only one in the house.

This was the last unexplainable event that occurred in the house.

HELEN, COME FORTH

Sarah Harrison

Business Owner

Asheville, North Carolina, 2009

This tale is one that teaches the lesson "be careful what you wish for," especially who you want to visit you from an otherworldly realm.

I'm the leader of a paranormal group in Asheville, North Carolina. The members of the Hickory, North Carolina group were visiting and wished to see a local, infamous haunt named "Helen's Bridge." We drove up Beaucatcher Mountain in two cars—my team in one, the Hickory group in another. The leader of the Hickory group had brought along his teenage brother. As we were exploring Helen's Bridge, the younger brother ran up and down the bridge yelling "Helen, come forth" over and over.

After a while, we decided to head down the mountain for spirits of another kind. I drove my car down first with the other car following. The people in my car saw nothing out of the ordinary. As we reached the bottom, the other car pulled over. Everyone in the second car was shaking and pale. The kid brother was wide-eyed and speechless for the first time that night. The story they told was chilling. As they were driving down the mountain, a woman came out of the woods. She had on a long dress and had long hair, but the worst part was her face. It was contorted and hideous, like something out of a horror movie. It was too grotesque to be a human being. They left swearing never to visit Helen's Bridge again.

I've returned to Helen's Bridge many times since that night. I've wondered if Helen was there, floating just out of reach of my senses. I do know I will never again say those three words, "Helen, come forth."

THE PLAYFUL GHOST

Steven J. Flowers

Air Traffic Control

Lancaster, New York, 2011

In 2011, I returned to my parents' house in my hometown to vacation for a week, which included the Fourth of July. I was excited to see family, friends, and participate in the town events. My parents had remodeled my old bedroom, so I slept in a spare bed set up in the main room of their finished basement. I was near a bar area, which was mostly being used to store old toys and decorations.

One toy was an old radio-controlled toy car with a Super Mario Kart video game character in it. The car was sitting on the counter of the bar. The first night, as I was laying there about to fall asleep, I thought I heard the rev of the toy's engine and heard it move a few inches on the bar. A few minutes later, I thought I heard the exact same thing again. I ignored it and eventually fell asleep.

The next morning, I was surprised to find the car on the floor next to the bar, as if it had driven itself off. I thought it was strange that I wasn't awoken by the rather large toy falling five feet onto a tile floor. I recalled having thought I heard the rev of the engine a couple of times before I fell asleep, but I had a busy day in front of me, so I set it back up on the bar, and the subject escaped my mind. The next evening, I arrived home just after midnight after having attended a town festival and visiting with old friends. I went to bed downstairs and glanced at the toy sitting on the counter.

Once again, I was almost asleep when I heard the engine rev and the toy move a few inches forward on the bar. This time the incident did get more of my attention as I recalled this happening the previous night. I still did not get out of bed to investigate, but I laid there with my eyes open, now focused on the noise and movement. About one minute later, the engine made a louder and longer, continuous rev; the toy drove at its top speed all the way down and then off of the bar! This caused me to jump out of bed as it was a shocking, undeniable event which happened right in front of me!

I started to investigate, hoping to find an obvious explanation. I thought perhaps my sister or parents were in the basement playing a joke on me. They were not. I checked to see if the power buttons were active on either the toy or the remote, that somehow it was transmitting the direction to accelerate despite nobody pushing the remote's acceleration button. Though there were still batteries in both the car and remote, both devices were clearly switched off.

The car is still in the basement, though it is now packed away out of sight.

ROADSIDE ASSISTANCE

Susan Bosman

Medical Field

Germantown, Wisconsin, 1979

I was driving home in a blizzard at night as I approached an intersection where a tavern, an old log cabin, a church, and an old cemetery were located. I was out in the country where three roads cross. The snow was almost blinding, but I could see the outline of a person waving his arms up and down frantically. I thought the person was trying to warn me that there was an accident at the intersection. If this was the case, I needed to help out as we were in the middle of nowhere.

I pulled my car quickly over to the side, and it slid into the ditch. I was scared, but knew I could run to the accident scene to get help. I hurried over to the intersection in the deep, deep snow to find there was no man, not even footprints, just silence and the flakes of falling snow. I was enraged as I felt someone had played a senseless trick on me. I went back to my car and was able to rock it back and forth to get out of the ditch.

A decade later, I attended a church in the same intersection for the grand opening of a museum of local history. Taped to the front door was a news article from approximately five years earlier saying that motorists should be aware of a ghost who plays with the traffic in the intersection! For 10 years, I had been mad, thinking some mean person had played a trick on me that winter's night. This ghost allegedly also ventures into a tavern in the intersection and throws dishes around. After reading this article, I was almost embarrassed that I had been so angry at the stranger, now knowing it was a ghost!

A SYNCHRONISTIC EULOGY

Tadd Everett McDivitt

Tour Guide and Researcher

Asheville, North Carolina, 2008

Webster's Dictionary defines synchronicity as "The coincidental occurrence of events and especially psychic events (as similar thoughts in widely separated persons or a mental image of an unexpected event before it happens) that seem related but are not explained by conventional mechanisms of causality—used especially in the psychology of C. G. Jung."

When paranormal enthusiasts and experts talk about manifestations, they are usually referring to clear documentation of the impossible. Photographs of spirits, footage of orbs, and other unexplainable plasmic phenomena are some of the most popular and sought after documentation of the paranormal. However, what if the paranormal has the capacity to be far more subtle? What if someone has a paranormal experience that is less about a tangible manifestation, and more about a sequence of "coincidences" so improbable that Pascal's laws of probability seem to be completely suspended?

During the summer of 2007, I had a friend staying with me who was a high-school senior, whom I will refer to as "Nathan." Nathan had been kicked out of his grandparents' home, as they had discovered that he was homosexual and disagreed with what they deemed "his lifestyle choices." At the time, I was an assistant manager at a movie theatre, and Nathan was one of our concessionists. He was mere months from graduation, so I decided to let him crash on my couch and maintain some semblance of stability to facilitate his graduation from high school. It was during these few months that Nathan had a death in the family. His grandfather, (from the other side of his family) had passed away suddenly. He was in a bad state, as he had effectively lost both of his grandfathers (one from death and one from a disagreement) in a few weeks. Nathan was a good kid who has grown into an intelligent and well-mannered man, but at the time he needed a confidant who would just listen. Like many people, we decided to let nature help clear his heavy heart, so we went hiking.

There is a valley in the Pisgah National Forest in western North Carolina's Smokey Mountains called "Graveyard Fields." There was a fire in the area decades ago, and even though there is new growth, it is much shorter, so you occasionally see the stumps of the giant trees that once towered over the area. The striking contrast of landscape from the dense forest that surrounds it is what earns the name "Graveyard Fields." From a distance, the stumps look like gravestones as far as the eye can see. A stream cuts through the valley, culminating in an impressive waterfall at the deepest base of the valley's dip. There are several Cherokee myths and legends about the stream and valley. It is said that the whole area is auspicious to communing with spirits (which, in my experiences, it most certainly is).

Nathan and I walked along the path that runs parallel to the stream, walking out to the shore where the terrain permitted. Nathan recalled memories and recounted stories about his grandfather as we walked. It was as if I was to be the lone audience of his heartfelt eulogy of sorts. Nathan mentioned that he had come to the area many times, as his grandfather was an avid camper. He continued to explain that his grandfather was actually a Boy Scout Troop Master and had taken numerous trips out to Graveyard Fields in his many years of youth mentoring. It was during one of these descriptions of Nathan's grandfather's camping techniques that I saw a glint in the water.

The sensation I experience when I "feel the mojo" is difficult to describe. It's as if time slows down and I have extra time to process information. I often instinctively cock my head to the side when I experience this sensation. The gesture is reflexive, as I'm intentionally viewing the world "sideways" to help fade my normal senses. There is a tingling sensation that overcomes my right shoulder as the prod to my senses demands, "Pay attention!"

This very sensation came over me as my mind became curious about the source of the glistening reflection in the bed of the stream before me. I cocked my head slightly to the right as I waded into the water and fished out the source of the reflection. It was a Swiss Army knife. I called to my companion, "Hey, look what I found!" as I waded to the shore. By the time I had reached the bank of the stream, about 15 feet across and about two feet deep at that point, Nathan had walked up, curious to see what I had found. I handed him the knife. He said to me, "Oh, wow! My grandfather lost one of these out here when I was a little kid." And as he unfolded the blade of the knife, there was, engraved on the blade, his grandfather's full name.

To many people, this story is just a highly improbable coincidence, and they are right. It's the kind of coincidence that makes me feel that Pascal's bell curve of probability has just been made the casualty of a skeet shoot. No glowing apparition appeared. No balls of plasma manifested themselves, challenging the laws of physics—just one, intense and incredibly emotionally significant coincidence. This is the kind of experience that I believe Carl Jung was talking about when he contrived the principle of "synchronicity." I like to keep this memory close, to remind myself that the paranormal isn't just about the documentation of the unexplainable "special effects." It also reminds me that sometimes such an experience seems to be intended for the select few that will see personal significance within the events.

THE LEGEND OF RED BLOOD ROCK

Thomas Vance Pollock

Driver

Mitchell County, North Carolina, 1881

As I was growing up, I remember often hearing my mother recount a local legend from her small mountain community. The tale spoke of a murdered man, fallen and bleeding, left to die on a great, pale boulder along the side of a creek, and although the body is long gone, every time it rains the boulder will still run red with blood! As a boy, this story always fascinated me, and I never tired of hearing it.

Many years later, I came across a publication while doing research on my great-great-grandfather, Kit Byrd. According to the book, he was murdered back in 1881, during a run-in with his "business partners" (i.e. fellow moonshiners), the Whitson brothers. The murder happened near Red Hill, a rural mountain community in Mitchell County, North Carolina. It is supposed that all three brothers fired shots at Kit as he attempted to walk away from a heated argument. Kit staggered to a nearby creek bank where he fell upon a large, pale boulder and bled to death.

Red Hill is just miles down the road from the community in which my mom grew up, so without knowing it, she had, for decades, been recounting a legend born from the murder of her own great-grandfather!

THE WHISPERING

Darrin Pearson

Security Coordinator

British Columbia, Canada, 1994

Life was tough as a textile salesman. I had to put up with picky clothing designers, but it was common for English-speaking Quebecers to work in such fields in the 1980s and 1990s. Finally one day, my sales manager asked me if I wanted to go to Vancouver, British Columbia, to service the western accounts. I couldn't pack fast enough; it was time for a fresh start. My marriage was stale, and I wanted to get my kids out of the political language hotspot where we currently lived.

It was the summer of 1994 and we were now living on the west coast, just getting by. I found a second job working security in the local film industry. It didn't take long before I was in charge of securing film locations, equipment, sets, and actors for various television shows like *The X-Files* and *Millennium*. The stories of one location called Riverview—a mental hospital that had been closed for 25 years—superseded it.

One night, the building rigger and myself started working on the third floor with the power off; the only light we had was that of our flashlights. Our hair would be on end as we walked past various rooms; you can only imagine the horrors that these poor souls went through while living here. We walked quickly, then on the second floor we experienced the same thing. Our senses were on fire, and all we wanted to do was run. Finally we reached the ground floor thinking we would soon be done, however we first had to walk through the east wing. As we walked to the end of a long, dark hallway, I sensed something like a soft kiss on my ear. I held my breath and kept walking. We entered a very large room with lots of windows that I assumed was a solarium. That's when my belief system changed forever. The room became alive with very subtle voices which seemed to completely surround us. My coworker and I stopped a foot apart. I couldn't breathe, as the pounding in my chest was so fierce. All I remember as we ran toward the exit was that the whispering seemed to follow us.

We still film there, and the many true stories that happen there are usually more intriguing than the stories being filmed.

THE TWISTED CROSS

Wyatt Carter III

Truck Driver

Port Hueneme, California, 1981–1982

Friends of mine had just bought a house that had a small guest house out back. I needed a place to live, and the guest house was perfect. My friends had two young boys, about 5 and 7 years old. The main house was small, built in the 1950s. The living room and kitchen were in the front, with bedrooms off a hallway in the back. It was a three-bedroom home, the last of which the boys would not go near and opted to share a single room instead. The unwanted third bedroom became a storage room for the family.

When I would visit in the main house, I'd enter through the back door and walk down the hallway past the bedrooms. It was summertime, but every time I walked by the unwanted room I felt cold—just by that door, nowhere else. Experiencing the consistently cold area always gave me a spooky feeling.

The boys were so afraid of the storage room, that they would go around the outside of the house to visit me, as opposed to walking down the hallway. One day I talked them into staying close to me as I opened the door to show them there was nothing scary in the room. I cracked the door open and air as cold as a freezer came out. I tried to stay calm as the children ran down the hall to their mom. She hugged the kids and brought her rosary beads to the storage room's door. There she hung them on the knob, saying they would ward off evil spirits, in hopes this would calm the boys. When I came to visit the next day, I noticed the rather large cross on the rosary was bent in half. The only way to have bent it would have been with pliers. I showed it to my friends and they were as upset as I was. There was a very uncomfortable and evil feeling exuding from the room from then on.

Shortly thereafter, I got into a serious motorcycle accident and nearly died. I wasn't sure if it was related to the strange occurrences in the house, but I was compelled to move. So were my friends. They put the house up for sale while living elsewhere while it sat vacant...for a year.

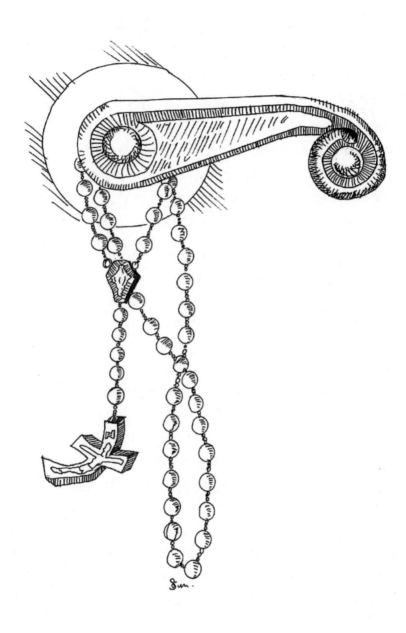

EPILOGUE

Well there you have it.

Can you truly meet a woman who mourned at President Lincoln's funeral? Can creatures that attack you in your nightmares truly leave hideous marks on your body? Can an alien truly appear then dematerialize right in front of you? Can your dog truly defend you from invisible things that lurk around a cemetery?

Obviously, if you ask certain people these questions, the answer will be a resounding "Yes!" And that is what makes a collection like this so fascinating. If even one of these stories is true, it is profound. That is because there is always an unsettling little gray area in life. Those are the spaces where mystery remains. It is easy for science and technology to make us feel as if all has been explained. Yet, ironically, science and technology advances only because we constantly discover new domains of possibility. The undiscovered, the unknown, is full of good things and bad things. Who knows how it will all turn out? But when we humans obtain our own little glimpses into those dark spaces, those dingy little cracks in reality, we often flinch like animals, reminded of how little we truly know in our mortal shells. From those glimpses, there is much to learn about the holographic and multi-layered form of this strange thing we call reality. Thus the flow of creepy little tales remains strong and never-ending. Keep them coming. I just threw another log on the fire!

GLOSSARY

annihilation The state of being destroyed into nothingness.

amorphous Shapeless or vague.

anomalous Irregular or unusual.

apparition A ghostlike figure that appears unexpectedly.

bemusement Confusion or disorientation.

berm A narrow ledge, usually at the top or bottom of a slope or along a riverbank.

bipedal Using two legs to walk on.

cryptozoology The study of mythical animals whose existence has not been confirmed.

disembodied Separated from the body.

dissipated Dispersed or scattered.

electroconvulsive Relating to the application of electric shocks to the brain.

emanate To come out from something; emit.

enmity Hostility, as toward an enemy.

epicenter The focal point of an unpleasant event.

malevolence The state of being evil or showing ill will.

manifest To make evident.

murder A group of crows.

myriad An indefinitely large number.

obliterated Destroyed or wiped out.

recessed Describing something, such as a door, that is set back into a wall.

reptilian Resembling a reptile.

rosary A set of prayers in the Catholic Church, or a string of beads used to keep count of those prayers.

translucent Describing a substance that allows light through; semitransparent.

viscera Internal organs, especially in the cavity of the torso, such as the intestines; the singular is viscus.

FOR MORE INFORMATION

American Institute of Parapsychology (AIP)

Executive Center

4131 NW 13th Street, Suite 208

Gainesville, FL 32609

Website: http://parapsychologylab.com

The AIP conducts research, educational courses, and consultations on all aspects of parapsychology, including apparitions, out-of-body experiences, extrasensory perception, and psychokinesis.

American Society for Psychical Research, Inc. (ASPR)

5 West 73rd Street

New York, NY 10023

(212) 799-5050

Website: http://www.aspr.com/

The ASPR is the oldest research organization for paranormal phenomena in the United States. One of its founders was psychologist William James, who studied human consciousness. The society continues to research how altered states of consciousness relate to matter, energy, and space.

Atlantic Paranormal Society (TAPS)

2362 West Shore Road

Warwick, RI 02889

Website: http://www.the-atlantic-paranormal-society.com

Founded in 1990, TAPS investigates claims of paranormal activity through research equipment and techniques. The group's work is featured on the SyFy series *Ghost Hunters.*

Committee for Skeptical Inquiry (CSI)

Box 703

Amherst, NY 14226

(716) 636-1425

E-mail: info@csicop.org

Website: http://www.csicop.org

The Committee for Skeptical Inquiry promotes research and inquiry into controversial paranormal claims. It also publishes articles and newsletters and holds conferences.

Parapsychology Foundation

P.O. Box 1562

New York, NY 10021

(212) 628-1550

E-mail: office@parapsychology.org

Website: http://www.parapsychology.org

The Parapsychology Foundation offers grants for the scientific investigation of psychic phenomena. It also publishes journals and books and sponsors lectures, outreach, and conferences.

Society of Paranormal Encounters of Canada, Training and Entity Research (S.P.E.C.T.E.R.)

77 Speedvale Avenue West, Apt. C

Guelph, ON N1H 1K1

Canada

Website: http://specterweb.tripod.com/guelph

S.P.E.C.T.E.R. investigates paranormal activities such as ghosts and hauntings across Southern Ontario using electromagnetic fields, infrared cameras, and other technology.

Society for Psychical Research (SPR)

49 Marloes Road

London W8 6LA

United Kingdom

0207 9378984

Website: http://www.spr.ac.uk/main/

The SPR investigates reports of extraordinary human experiences that cannot be explained by current scientific models. Members conduct research and share their findings in journals.

WEBSITES

Because of the changing nature of Internet links, Rosen Publishing has developed an online list of websites related to the subject of this book. This site is updated regularly. Please use this link to access this list:

http://www.rosenlinks.com/TTOT/Creep

FOR FURTHER READING

Argie, Theresa, and Eric Olsen. *America's Most Haunted: The Secrets of Famous Paranormal Places.* New York, NY: Berkley Books, 2014.

Balzano, Christopher, and Tim Weisberg. *Haunted Objects: Stories of Ghosts on Your Shelf.* Iola, WI: Krause Publications, 2012.

Belanger, Jeff. *Paranormal Encounters* (Haunted: Ghosts and the Paranormal). New York, NY: Rosen Publishing Group, 2012

Belanger, Jeff. *Real-Life Ghost Encounters.* (Haunted: Ghosts and the Paranormal). New York, NY: Rosen Publishing Group, 2013.

Goodwyn, Melba. *Chasing Graveyard Ghosts: Investigations of Haunted and Hallowed Ground.* Woodbury, MN: Llewellyn Publications, 2011.

Haughton, Brian. *Famous Ghost Stories.* (Haunted: Ghosts and the Paranormal). New York, NY: Rosen Publishing Group, 2012.

Henneberg, Susan. *Investigating Ghosts and the Spirit World* (Understanding the Paranormal). New York, NY: Britannica Educational Publishing, 2015.

James, M.R. *Collected Ghost Stories.* Oxford, England: Oxford University Press, 2011.

Newman, Rich. *The Ghost Hunter's Field Guide: Over 1000 Haunted Places You Can Experience.* Woodbury, MN: Llewellyn Publications, 2011.

Ogden, Tom. *Haunted Cemeteries: Creepy Crypts, Spine-Tingling Spirits, and Midnight Mayhem.* Guilford, CT: Globe Pequot Press, 2010.

Rogers, Lisa. *On Haunted Ground: The Green Ghost and Other Spirits of Cemetery Road.* Woodbury, MN: Llewellyn Publications, 2012.

Warren, Ed, and Lorraine Warren. *Ghost Hunters.* Los Angeles, CA: Graymalkin Media, 2014.

Wilder, Annie. *Trucker Ghost Stories: And Other True Tales of Haunted Highways, Weird Encounters, and Legends of the Road.* New York, NY: Tor Books, 2012.

INDEX

ABOUT THE AUTHOR

Joshua P. Warren travels the world investigating strange phenomena. For more than 20 years, he's published numerous books on all paranormal topics, including ghosts, UFOs, cryptids, ESP, and spirituality. Often called "Dr. Supernatural," in 2004, he made the cover of the science journal *Electric Space Craft* for his team's grueling work analyzing ghostly plasmas in nature. Warren has appeared on the History Channel, NatGeo, Discovery, Animal Planet, SyFy, TLC, and starred in the Travel Channel series *Paranormal Paparazzi*. He is frequently hired as a technical consultant by major production companies, such as Warner Brothers, and he helped produce the "Winchester House Experiment," for the *Ghost Adventures* TV show, voted best experiment in the program's history by fans.

Warren hosts the popular radio program *Speaking of Strange* and is also a correspondent for the *Coast to Coast AM* radio show. He is the creator and owner of the Asheville Mystery Museum in Asheville, North Carolina, where his original ghost tours and ghost hunts draw thousands from around the world each year. A self-proclaimed connoisseur of the creepy and "The Wizard of Weird," he divides his time between Asheville and Puerto Rico, where he operates the Bermuda Triangle Research Base.